The
HOT AIR BALLOON
Book

BUILD and LAUNCH
KONGMING LANTERNS, SOLAR TETROONS, AND MORE

CLIVE CATTERALL

CHICAGO
REVIEW
PRESS

Published by Chicago Review Press, Incorporated
814 North Franklin Street
Chicago, Illinois 60610
978-1-61374-096-5

Library of Congress Cataloging-in-Publication Data
Is available from the Library of Congress.

Cover design: Andrew Brozyna, AJB Design, Inc.
Interior design: Rattray Design

Printed in the United States of America
5 4 3 2 1

Contents

11. Troubleshooting and Other Information 211

For Cath

Introduction

How to Use This Book

Each project chapter in this book is split into two parts. The first part covers the design and science of the balloon. The second part contains the instructions for building.

You can build the balloons in any order you like; all of the instructions for a particular design should be contained within its own chapter. Start with an easy one, though—either the Basic Trash Bag Balloon (page 41) or the Kongming Lantern (page 71).

If you run into problems building these balloons, or if you cannot find the right materials, see the troubleshooting tips in chapter 11 (page 211). I have tried to gather all of the fixes and advice there.

Safety Note

All building and launching should be done under adult supervision. Many of the projects contain steps that use heat or sharp tools. If you have not used a particular tool before, ask someone to show you how to handle it safely. Wear appropriate safety equipment, especially heatproof gloves and safety glasses when handling containers of hot wax. Store your hot soldering iron in a proper stand when welding sheet plastic—***don't just lay it down.***

Read through the whole of chapter 2 before you launch your first balloon. Follow the safety advice and remember that safety is your responsibility. If you do not follow instructions and warnings, the balloons in this book can cause injuries or damage. The author and publisher accept no responsibility for damage or loss caused by anyone following the projects in this book.

1
Balloon History

Where Does the Balloon Come From?

Historians know that the first human-carrying balloon was designed and built by the Montgolfier brothers in France, and it flew for the first time in 1783. But the balloon was not a completely new idea, and it is very hard to find out who first thought of lifting things with a bag full of gas. In fact, there are a surprising number of different countries that claim to be the home of the inventor of the balloon.

China

The Chinese people love paper hot air balloons, and there are probably more paper hot air balloons flown in China than in the rest of the world combined.

The most common balloon used in festivals has a small, tapered envelope that has a square cross-section at the top that tapers to a round cross-section at the bottom. It is usually called a Kongming lantern rather than a balloon, because it has a small wax burner inside that produces a bright, luminous flame that lights up the whole envelope like a

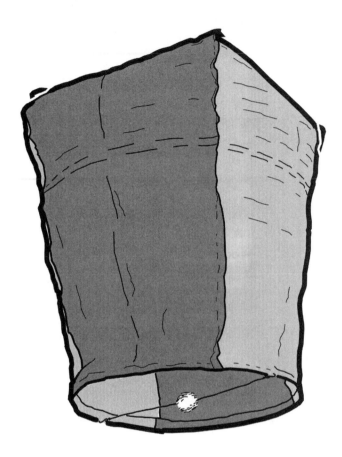

A Kongming lantern

Chinese lantern. The balloon was given the name *Kongming* after the man who is said to have invented it.

Zhuge Liang, also known as Kongming, was an advisor, military strategist, and chancellor for the Shu Han region during the Three Kingdoms period of Chinese history. He was famous for his wisdom, intelligence, and cunning. He was so clever that he could always invent new and surprising ways of beating his enemies—even when the situation looked impossible. One of the stories about Zhuge Liang tells how he invented the hot air balloon.

Zhuge Liang and his troops were occupying the town of Pingyang when his enemy Sima Yi surrounded it and began a siege, hoping to force the famous Zhuge Liang to surrender. Sima Yi's troops had occupied the land all around the town and watched carefully for messengers leaving the town, so there was no way for Zhuge Liang to send a signal to his allies for help.

Zhuge Liang noticed that the wind was blowing toward his allies, so he asked for a special large lantern to be made with no hole in the top and a wax burner held in the bottom. He painted a message onto the side of the lantern and carried it up to a tower on the town wall. He lit the burner and released the lantern, which floated away in the wind toward his allies. Sima Yi's troops below could only watch as the lantern passed overhead, carrying a message that asked for help. Sure enough, Zhuge Liang's allies saw the message, rode to Pingyang, and rescued Zhuge Liang and his troops.

Apart from this legend, there is no historical evidence that Zhuge Liang invented the hot air balloon. One writer suggested that the Kongming lantern might have been invented by a Chinese lantern-maker and then named after the famously clever Zhuge Liang, perhaps because it looks a lot like the little square hat Zhuge Liang always used to wear. Sadly, even this explanation is unlikely as there are no written descriptions of paper hot air balloons in China before 1783.

Italy

Francesco Lana was born in 1631 in Brescia, Lombardy, an area in the north of modern Italy. He became a Jesuit priest and, like many Jesuits, was encouraged to study so that he could become a teacher. Eventually he became a professor of mathematics and physics at Brescia, and while he was teaching there he learned about Otto Von Guericke's experiments at Regensburg and Magdeburg in 1654.

Von Guericke had shown that two copper hemispheres 20 inches (50 cm) in diameter could be held together by pumping out the air from the space between them. The atmospheric pressure outside the hemispheres was so great that once all the air had been pumped out, two teams of eight horses could not pull them apart.

Lana was fascinated by the experiment, but he was particularly interested in the new and more efficient vacuum pump Von Guericke had invented. Lana calculated the weight that must have been lost from the pair of copper hemispheres when the air was pumped out. If a sphere could be made from thin enough material, then the weight of the air removed from inside the sphere by this new pump might actually be greater than the weight of the sphere itself. This should make the sphere float in the air!

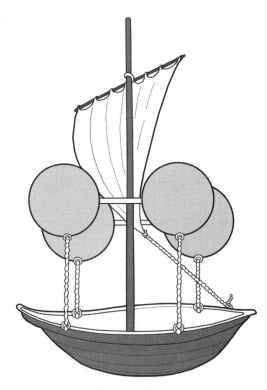

Lana's airboat

In 1663 Lana designed a lighter-than-air ship, the details of which he later published in 1670 in his book *Prodomo*. This design used four large floating copper spheres from which a boat is suspended. The boat had a sail and hull, as Lana intended it to be propelled by the wind and steered much as a boat on the sea.

Lana never tried to build his airboat, and of course there would have been practical problems if he had. To make the airboat fly, I estimate that the copper skin of the big spheres would have to be less than 0.004 inches (0.1 mm) thick. This is about the thickness of a human hair and only about four times the thickness of household aluminum foil. At this thickness, the sphere would collapse under its own weight even before you tried to pump out any air.

Portugal and Brazil

Bartholomeu Lourenço de Gusmão was born in Sao Paolo, Brazil, in 1685. At that time Brazil was a part of the Portuguese empire, so when it became clear that Gusmão was a brilliant student and had quickly outgrown the opportunities for study in Brazil, it was natural that he should travel all the way to Portugal to study at the University of Coimbra. At Coimbra he studied mathematics, physics, chemistry, astronomy, and philology (the language of literature). It must have been during these studies that Gusmão discovered the work of Francesco Lana, and Gusmão began to develop Lana's ideas for flying machines.

Gusmão knew that Lana's copper spheres would not be practical, but his early attempts at designing a flying machine used equally strange devices to lift the boat, such as powerful magnets.

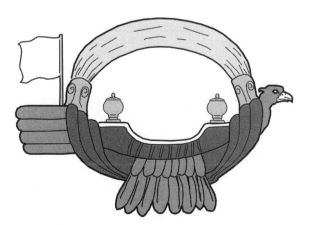

Gusmão's magnetic airboat *Passarola*

Some say that Gusmão observed a soap bubble rising in the hot air above a candle flame and realized that hot air was the source of lift he was looking for. Whatever the source of his inspiration, in 1709 he asked if he could demonstrate a model of a flying machine to King John V of Portugal. Over the course of three days he made three separate demonstrations in front of the royal court, where "he propelled a ball up to the roof by combustion."

We don't know how Gusmão's model worked, but some writers believe that it was a paper hot air balloon, maybe even with a small burner fixed to the opening at the bottom. If this is true, then Gusmão produced a working model hot air balloon 73 years before the Montgolfier brothers. Unfortunately, he did not write down exactly how either his demonstration or his new design for an airboat worked.

Sadly, Gusmão did not live to complete his airboat. The Inquisition started to investigate him in 1724, and rather than face any charges, he fled to Toledo in Spain. He died of a fever only weeks after he arrived.

Scotland

The 18th century was a time of rapid development in chemistry and physics. Earlier researchers such as Robert Boyle and Robert Hooke had investigated the physical properties of air. But scientists like the Scotsman Joseph Black, the Englishmen Henry Cavendish and Joseph Priestley, and the Frenchman Antoine Lavoisier were now interested in the chemical properties of individual gases rather than the mixture that makes up air.

Joseph Black was Professor of Medicine at Glasgow University but lectured in chemistry as well. In 1766, Black read a paper written by Henry Cavendish that described new gases that Cavendish had isolated. One gas was particularly odd. Cavendish called it "inflammable air" because you could actually burn the gas in air. Almost as strange was its very low density: 13 liters of the new gas weighed the same as only 1 liter of ordinary air. We know this gas today as hydrogen.

Black knew the low density meant that a light bag filled with the new gas might just be able to float in the air. This would be a superb demonstration for his students—it would really show off the properties of the new gas. But what to use for the bag? Paper was no good because the gas passed right through it.

For hundreds of years, pig bladders had been used to make balloons and lightweight balls for games, so Black went to the local butcher's shop. Rather than a pig bladder, which would have been a bit small, Black chose an *allantois* from a butchered cow. An allantois is a long, sausage-shaped membrane that is both strong and gas-tight.

Back at his home, Black filled the allantois with Cavendish's new gas and tied off the opening. While curious visitors to Black's house watched, the allantois floated up to the ceiling and stayed there.

France

Historians don't know the exact date when Joseph Montgolfier had the idea of building a device carried into the sky with the lift from hot air. One story says that in 1777, Joseph watched laundry being dried over a fire and being lifted up by the hot air. We also know that Joseph had read a French translation of Cavendish's paper that described hydrogen for the first time.

In November 1782, Joseph heard about the problem of assaulting the fortress of Gibraltar, where all attempts to storm the fortress by normal means had failed. While thinking about this problem, Joseph started to wonder if troops could be carried up the cliffs using the same force that made cinders and embers fly up into the air above a bonfire.

To test his idea, he built a lightweight box. Rather than make solid flat panels, which would be too heavy, he made a wooden frame from thin sticks and covered the sides and top with taffeta, a very fine fabric made from silk. The box was 1 meter wide and 1 meter long by about 1.3 meters tall (about 3 feet by 3 feet by 4 feet), and open at the bottom.

Underneath the open bottom Joseph crumpled some paper, which he lit to make a small fire. After a short while, the box rose into the air and bumped into the ceiling of his room.

After Joseph had demonstrated the model to his brother Etienne, they set about making a model three times as large. On December 14, 1782, they tested this larger model and the lift was so strong that it broke away and flew for 2 kilometers (1.2 miles) before landing in a field.

They made larger and more ambitious balloons during 1783, first demonstrating a small balloon in front of the public at Annonay (where they lived) and eventually demonstrating a giant balloon in front of the king and queen at Versailles. The balloon that they flew for the king even had live passengers—a duck, a sheep, and a rooster. These were intended to test the effects of flying on live animals before a human took to the air.

As soon as news reached Paris about the demonstration at Annonay, the physicist Jacques Charles started work on his own balloon design. Throughout 1783 there was a race between the Montgolfier brothers and Charles to design a balloon that could lift humans safely into the air. Charles wanted to use Henry Cavendish's hydrogen gas rather than hot air and built a number of test balloons made from fabric coated in a rubber solution.

During October 1783, Pilatre de Rozier tested a new, larger Montgolfier balloon. The Montgolfiers had built it for the first human flight and, because the demonstration would be in front of the king, had decorated it with portraits of the king, signs of the zodiac, and fleurs-de-lis. It was 23 meters (75 feet) tall and 15 meters (50 feet) in diameter, weighed 780 kg (about 1,700 pounds), and held 2,000 cubic meters (more than 70,000 cubic feet) of air. For the tests, it was filled with hot air from a large bonfire on the ground and securely tethered using long ropes, yet despite this, de Rozier's balloon was able to rise to a height of 99 meters (325 feet) in less than 15 seconds. As soon as these tests were complete, the Montgolfiers began the work to fit an iron brazier to the balloon so it could carry its own fire while it flew. By feeding the fire with wood and straw, de Rozier would be able to fly much farther than earlier balloons, which were simply held over a bonfire to fill with hot air before being released. Jacques Charles's final balloon was also under construction all through November, and it was only days away from flying when de Rozier launched the giant Montgolfier balloon.

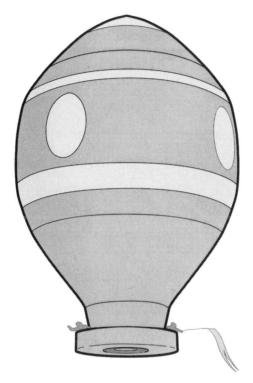

The Montgolfiers' balloon

On November 21, 1783, Pilatre de Rozier and the Marquis d'Arlandes took off in the Montgolfier balloon from the Chateau de la Muette. The first manned free flight in a balloon lasted only 25 minutes and covered 9 kilometers (5.6 miles), from the Chateau de la Muette, near the Bois de Boulogne, to the windmills on the Butte aux Cailles on the outskirts of Paris. The balloon had plenty of remaining fuel and could have flown four or five times as far, but de Rozier brought the balloon down because burning embers from the fire had scorched holes in the envelope and it had started to smolder.

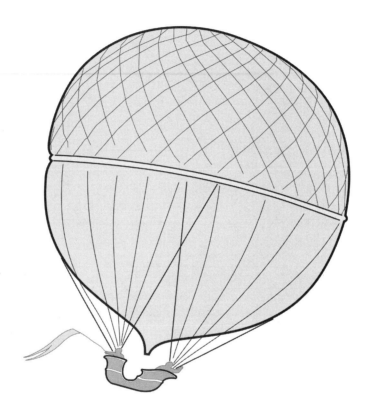

Jacques Charles's balloon

It is interesting that the first manned balloon flight should end in this way, as it shows why hot air balloons were abandoned shortly after that historic first flight. Although it was far easier to make a hot air balloon—it did not need to be sealed and filled with expensive hydrogen gas—burning embers often rose into the envelope and started small fires. De Rozier himself was killed less than two years later in 1785 when the envelope of his balloon caught fire as he attempted to cross the English Channel.

So Who *Did* Invent the Balloon?

To my mind, the true home of the balloon is France. The idea of the balloon was certainly around already, and some people had already demonstrated little models of flying balloons—Bartholomeu de Gusmão, Black, maybe even an unknown Chinese lantern maker.

But nobody doubts that the balloon that allowed mankind to fly free in the sky for the first time was made by the Montgolfier brothers in France. They solved all of the technical problems, organized the manufacture of the balloon, and demonstrated it in front of a large audience. Joseph Montgolfier, in particular, took the vague ideas about lighter-than-air craft that had been floating around the scientific world for over 150 years and used them to make a working model. It was an amazing achievement.

Celebrations and Festivals

From prehistoric times, mankind has looked up at the sky with wonder. For prehistoric man the sun seemed to disappear into the ground, and then, out of the growing blackness of the sky, stars magically appeared. Sometimes meteors streaked down to the ground. Many of the early myths and legends tried to explain the mysteries of the natural world and, by explaining them, take away fear of the unknown.

It is no surprise that as soon as people learned how to make balloons, the idea of sending a light into the sky became important to them. Wherever the technology of balloon-making traveled, people adapted their festivals and celebrations to include balloons.

No people have taken the balloon to their hearts more than the Chinese. During the autumn festival in China, people write their hopes and wishes for the coming year onto the side of a paper Kongming lantern. The lanterns are released during the festival to carry people's wishes to the ancestors who live in the sky.

The people of Thailand also love paper hot air balloons. During November they hold a festival called Loi Krathong, where they give thanks for clean water. Small floating lanterns are made by placing a candle inside a cup of banana leaves, and during the festival hundreds are released to form a carpet of light that floats down the river. But in the north of Thailand they hold the Pi Yeng festival as well.

Rather than simply make lanterns that float on the water, they make lanterns that float on the air—Khom Loi, or paper hot air balloons. These are released in the late evening in huge numbers, filling the sky with hundreds of new stars to carry away bad luck and ill fortune.

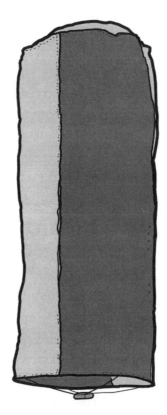

A Khom Loi

But hot air balloons are not always a successful addition to festivals. In Rio de Janeiro, the people follow the Portuguese tradition of releasing paper hot air balloons during the June festivals to celebrate the lives of St. Anthony, St. Paul, and St. John. Over time the balloons have become larger and larger, trailing giant religious images or portraits of sports stars along with huge strings of fireworks. After a number of forest fires, near misses with aircraft, and damage to cars and houses, the authorities in Rio finally banned the giant hot air balloons in 1998.

But the balloon-builders did not stop. Since the ban, there has been an annual cat-and-mouse game in which the craftsmen who build these giant paper balloons take part in elaborate schemes to launch from secret locations, racing away from the launch site as soon as the balloon is airborne. Crowds of locals and tourists still gather to watch the balloons light up the sky. Large teams of police officers are forced to spend all night during the festivals trying to catch these *baloeiros*, or balloon men. The punishment for *baloeiros* who get caught is severe—up to five years in prison.

Spying for the Army

In the modern world of military satellites and spy drones, it is hard to understand that back in the 18th century it was sometimes difficult to pinpoint the position of an enemy army to within 100 miles (160 km). Because you can see a long way in flat country from a balloon, it is not very surprising that balloons were used by military commanders right from the start. The French army set up a balloon corps only four years after the first manned balloon flight.

Observers were hoisted up by balloon to locate the enemy and report back down to the commander. Usually the balloon was fixed to the ground by a long rope so it didn't drift away, and there was some method of sending messages from the balloon basket to the ground.

By the time of the American Civil War, artillery commanders had realized that the balloon gave them the opportunity to greatly improve the accuracy of artillery. By reporting the actual position of shell landings, the artillerymen could adjust the aim of their guns to land the shells exactly on target. Because of this, infantrymen hated these balloons and would try to shoot them down as soon as they appeared, frequently mistaking their own balloons for those of the enemy. The Union Army started making balloons decorated with the stars and stripes, so at least their own troops would not shoot at them.

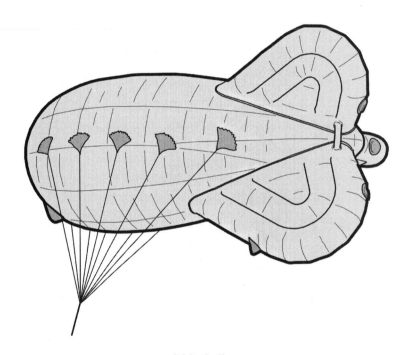

A kite balloon

By the time of the First World War, new balloons were being used that were part balloon and part kite in design, so they were stable even in high winds. The observers had high-powered cameras, binoculars, and even telephones so they could speak directly to the artillery batteries and to headquarters. But the arrival of the airplane marked the end of fixed observer balloons in warfare, as they were too vulnerable to airplane attack.

Steerable Balloons

For the military, a free-flying balloon has one major drawback: you cannot control where it goes. The envelope of a balloon has to be big to lift even one soldier, and it takes a lot of power to push that envelope through the air. Early designs of military balloons showed sails and rudders, oars, paddle wheels, and propellers. None of these schemes had any hope of working. It was not until the development of light and powerful internal combustion engines in the late 19th century that it was possible to make a balloon that could drive itself in any direction.

The first practical steerable balloon, or *dirigible*, was built by the wealthy Brazilian adventurer Alberto Santos-Dumont in France. In 1901 he won the prestigious Deutsch prize awarded by the Aero Club for a half-hour controlled flight around the Eiffel Tower in his *Number 6*.

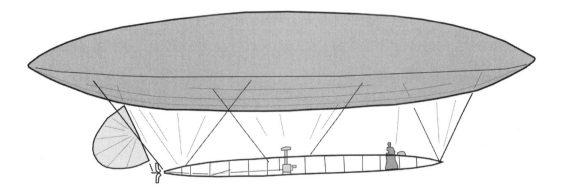

The Santos-Dumont *Number 6*

But it is the Germans who are remembered for developing the powered steerable balloon into a sophisticated airship: the zeppelin. Zeppelins made scheduled flights around the world and across the Atlantic Ocean. There was even a plan to allow them to dock with a special tower mounted on the top of the Empire State Building, allowing passengers to fly right into the middle of Manhattan.

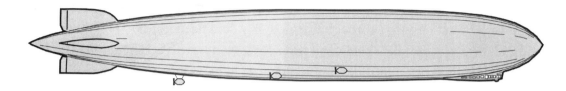

The *Graf Zeppelin*

Balloons as Weapons

Even before the Union Army started to use balloon observation to direct artillery fire, the Austrians had tried to use balloons to bomb the enemy directly. It must have seemed obvious that if the wind was blowing in the right direction, they could simply tie bombs to a balloon and float them over enemy lines.

The trouble is that the wind has a habit of changing direction just at the wrong moment. This is what happened to the Austrians when they laid siege to Venice in 1849. They built 200 small balloons, each carrying a 24- or 30-pound (11 or 14 kg) bomb, and the plan was that the bombs would drop onto the city when a time fuse ran out. Unfortunately, once the balloons had been released, the wind reversed direction and the balloons floated back over the Austrian lines. The bombs began dropping on Austrian troops, leaving Venice virtually undamaged.

The problem with balloon bombs is that you need a reliable wind and a really big target. It is impossible to tell exactly where a balloon bomb will land, so it is almost impossible to damage anything strategically important. But in the 20th century, war was waged against the civilian population just as much as it was waged against enemy troops. If you

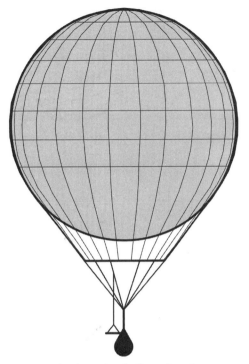

An Austrian balloon bomb

just want to terrorize an enemy country, then you can use balloon bombs, because most will end up injuring random civilians.

During the Second World War, many British cities were surrounded by barrage balloon defenses. Barrage balloons were large and shaped just like the kite balloon pictured earlier, but they were moored using a thick steel cable. It was the cable, rather than the balloon, that would do the damage to enemy aircraft. If an airplane flew into the cable, it could slice off a wing or cut the fuselage right down the middle.

In September 1939 a large number of barrage balloons broke away from their moorings during a storm. Because of the direction of the wind, the balloons trailed across Finland,

Denmark, and Germany. They caused damage to railways and power lines and even destroyed a radio station. Inspired by this incident, the British started Operation Outward. This was a program to deliberately release thousands of small balloons carrying a small bomb with a time fuse or a packet of propaganda leaflets, or trailing a 300-foot-long (92 meter) steel wire.

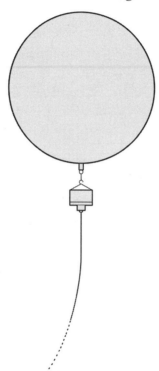

A wire-trailing Operation Outward balloon

It was the steel wires that led to the most spectacular success of this operation. In 1942, balloons trailing steel wires shorted out power lines outside Leipzig and caused fires that burned the Böhlen power station to the ground.

The second major use of the balloon as a weapon also occurred in the Second World War. In 1942, the US Air Force bombed Tokyo, showing that even Japan's capital was not out of reach of the war. The Japanese were desperate to retaliate against the mainland

United States and devised a plan to use balloon bombs carried by high-level winds called *jet streams*. These are strong winds that circulate around the world in fairly fixed patterns but only between 30,000 and 38,000 feet (9,200 and 11,600 meters). During certain parts of the year, a powerful jet stream travels at up to 200 mph (320 kph) from Japan to the United States. The Japanese built a sophisticated balloon that could adjust its own buoyancy to keep it flying at the right height to sit in this wind. Because of the speed of the wind, the balloon bombs were carried from Japan to the United States in just three days.

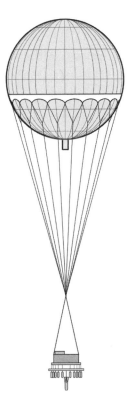

A Japanese balloon bomb

From November 1944 to April 1945, the Japanese released 9,300 of these balloons, of which it is believed only 285 reached the United States. Although only five people were killed by the balloon bombs, the US government took them very seriously. All reports of balloon bombs were suppressed, and through careful detective work, the manufacturing and launch sites were identified and bombed. Because the Japanese military had heard no reports of damage, they thought that the balloon bombs were not working and did not bother to rebuild the factories.

UFOs

The famous 18th-century scientist Jacques Charles launched the first unmanned gas balloon on August 27, 1783, only 12 weeks after the Montgolfier brothers demonstrated their unmanned hot air balloon. History remembers the Montgolfier balloon, but Charles's balloon was a first as well.

Charles flew his gas balloon from the Champ de Mars in Paris, with an audience of 6,000 rich guests who had paid for a seat to watch this marvel. The balloon took off in front of the astonished crowd and flew for 45 minutes, covering a distance of 15 miles (24 km). It landed in a field belonging to the village of Gonesse. The villagers had not heard of the demonstration and were terrified by this giant flapping monster descending from the sky. Thinking that some devil had fallen from the sky intending to carry them all away, they attacked the balloon with pitchforks, hooks, and scythes, cutting the envelope to shreds.

And there it is: Jacques Charles was responsible for the very first UFO sighting caused by a balloon.

Over the next 200 years, balloons were responsible for many UFO sightings—some deliberate, like the 2009 Morristown sightings, and some accidental, like the 1947 Roswell incident.

During the 1950s and 1960s, you could regularly find ads in the back pages of magazines like *Popular Science* for ready-made hot air balloons 9 or 10 feet (2.7 or 3.0 meters) tall made from a variety of materials, and *Popular Mechanics* published plans to make your own tissue paper balloon. During the same period the same magazines published articles suggesting that many UFO sightings were caused by weather balloons. It did not take long for people to start creating their own UFO hoaxes.

2

How to Fly Your Balloon

All of the balloons in this book are large enough to cause problems for low-flying aircraft, and many carry a small burner that can set buildings and crops alight, so you do need to follow a few safety rules. *Remember that you are responsible for any damage your balloon causes*, so you need to take care.

Safety Rules

1. Keep free-flying model balloons smaller than 6 feet (1.8 m) in size. You have to register balloons over 6 feet with the Federal Aviation Administration.
2. Never fly balloons within 3 miles (4.8 km) of an airfield.
3. Make sure the burner is fixed securely.
4. Never fly balloons during a drought or in late summer. If your balloon comes down too early, the burner could still be lit, and if it hasn't rained for a long time, the grass and standing crops are easier to set on fire.

5. Coat the bottom 12 inches (30 cm) of a tissue paper balloon with fire retardant. You must apply the fire retardant before you use the paper to create a balloon (see chapter 11, page 221).

6. Put the lid back on your fuel bottle before you light the burner. Bottles are easy to kick over.

7. Take care with alcohol burners—the flame is almost invisible in sunlight.

8. Use a lighter rather than matches. You can use a lighter with one hand, and there are no smoldering matches to throw away.

9. Keep a pair of pliers or wire cutters in your back pocket when launching a balloon. If the wind picks up or you want to abandon the launch after you have lit the burner, you can quickly cut the burner wires and stamp out the burner.

10. If at any time the balloon itself catches fire, you should let go of it and step away. Do not try to put the fire out—you will not save the balloon and you may burn yourself. Just make sure the balloon doesn't set fire to anything else.

11. Make sure you can quickly put out any fires that your balloon may start. It is a good idea to have a bucket of water nearby when you launch.

12. Never try to fly a fire balloon indoors.

13. Keep all pets away from your balloon.

14. Get permission to fly balloons over private land and to retrieve them when they come down.

15. Always follow your balloon. You might be able to reuse the balloon, but more important, you might have to stamp out a small fire or call the fire department.

You also need to be familiar with the laws in your area relating to hot air balloons. In the United States, federal regulations covering balloons are contained in a document called "Title 14 CFR 101 Moored Balloons, Kites, Unmanned Rockets, and Unmanned Free Balloons." The latest version should be available online if you search for "Title 14 CFR 101." In addition, some state and local governments have their own rules regarding model aircraft, so check with local law enforcement to find out what you can and cannot do.

Weather

All model hot air balloons are made from the thinnest and lightest materials available so that they can lift more strongly. But this also makes the balloon fragile and easy to damage, so you need to check the weather before you launch.

Never fly when it's going to rain. Even a brief rain shower will destroy a tissue paper balloon.

Launch on a day with little or no wind. Wind chills the balloon and can push the flame onto the paper sides of the balloon. The stronger the wind, the better your shelter needs to be.

To launch a solar balloon you need clear sky with no clouds or haze. Launch from a sheltered position in full sun. If there is any wind, you may need to jump-start the balloon using a blow-dryer (see the section on launching tetroons later in this chapter, page 39).

Choose Your Launch Site

Most model balloon accidents happen during launching. Choosing the right place to launch your balloon can make a big difference.

If you want your balloon to fly over a particular place, you need to launch from a point that is directly upwind. The wind at ground level swirls around trees and buildings, so you need to move to a large open space to get a true idea of the wind direction. You can also look at a flag or weather vane on the top of a tall building.

Your launch site must provide shelter from the wind. You need to find something that is tall and wide enough so that the wind does not spill around it and push the balloon about while it is heating up. Buildings, fences, and brick walls are good, but hedges often let too much wind through. Add extra windbreaks if the wind can still get to the balloon. Any large object can be put near the balloon to help, but choose something that will not catch fire if the balloon burns up.

Check downwind to see if your balloon might hit anything after you launch it. The balloon will be carried along with the wind as it climbs, so there should not be any trees, buildings, or power lines in the way. Remember, the stronger the wind, the farther your balloon will fly before it can climb to a safe height.

Solar Power Meter

If you are going to launch a solar balloon, you need to know if the sun is strong enough to keep it flying. Because this is mostly determined by the cloud cover and haze, it is difficult to give any advice. The best way to check whether the sun has enough power to fly your balloon is to measure it directly. If you have access to photovoltaic solar cells, either on your house to generate electricity or from the science department of your school, you can use these to measure the solar power. Silicon photovoltaic cells are most sensitive to the red end of the spectrum, which is ideal for measuring the heating effect from the sun.

If you don't have photovoltaic cells, you can make a simple solar power meter out of a plastic trash bag, two thermometers, string, and cardboard:

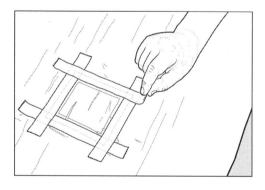

1. Cut a rectangular hole about 4 inches (10 cm) square halfway down the trash bag. Cut a 6-inch (15 cm) square from a clear polyethylene bag and tape the clear square over the hole. Make sure the tape pieces cross over to stop any leaks.

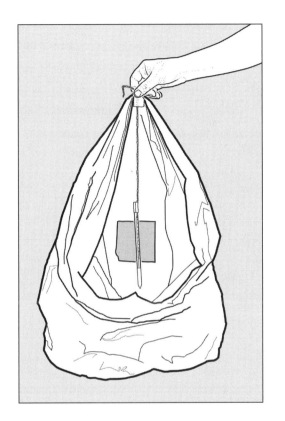

2. Attach one of the thermometers to a length of string using tape. Lower the thermometer into the trash bag and tape the string to the top edge of the trash bag so that the scale of the thermometer is level with the clear window.

3. Cut circle of heavy corrugated cardboard from a pizza box or similar so that it will just fit into the trash bag and hold the bottom open.

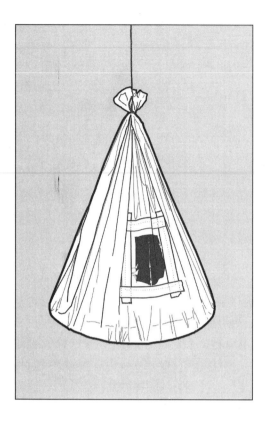

4. Gather the top of the bag around the string and tape it closed. Hang up the power meter by the string so it is in full sun but out of the wind. Hang up the second thermometer in the shade.

After 15 minutes, take readings from both thermometers. *If the temperature in the power meter is more than 36°F (20°C) higher than the temperature in the shade, then you can launch your Solar Tetroon.* Larger tetroons can launch with a slightly lower temperature rise.

This solar power meter is very sensitive to the wind. Any wind will make the temperature lower in the power meter than it would be in a real balloon. If it is windy, you could try hanging the solar power meter indoors behind a window but in full sun, and put the second thermometer in the same room but out of the sun.

Launching Equipment

Along with fuel and a lighter, you will need a pair of pliers and a pair of launching poles to get your balloons off the ground. Launching poles are blunt-ended sticks that support the balloon from the inside while it fills with hot air, leaving your hands free to keep the tissue paper away from the flame.

Bamboo garden canes are ideal, as they are strong and thin and easy to push into the ground. However, because they are thin, they also tend to poke holes through the tissue paper. To fix this you need to put small plastic drink bottles, jam jars, or empty soft drink cans over the ends to make the poles blunt.

If you want to make a more permanent pair of launching poles, fold a 6-inch (15 cm) length of garden hose in half, slip one leg of the hose over a bamboo cane, and tape it into place.

If you have problems with the wind collapsing the tissue paper onto the burner, you can use extra garden canes to hold the paper back (as in the illustration on page 27). These canes should be much shorter and pushed into the ground on either side of the launching poles. When the balloon is dropped into place, the burner should sit in the center of the circle.

Always keep a pair of pliers or wire cutters in your back pocket when launching a fire balloon. If the wind picks up or you want to abandon the launch for any reason, you can cut the burner wires, let the burner drop away, and stamp it out. You can always fit another burner and launch when the wind is calmer.

Luminous Flames

If you want to launch your balloon at night, you need to use a fuel that produces a luminous flame. Alcohol burners produce a lot of heat, but the flame is a very pale blue and produces almost no light. With care, alcohol can be used for daytime launches. However, the flame is almost invisible in sunlight, so setting fire to spills is a particular danger: the spills can be burning strongly before you realize something is wrong.

Kerosene is an ideal fuel. It is widely available, cheap, and produces a bright yellow flame. The only disadvantage is that it makes a lot of soot when it burns. Although this coats the inside of the envelope, you can usually reuse the envelope if you recover it. Diesel fuel and heating oil also work well.

Wax melted down from candles is a good source of fuel for the solid burners. Because the wax was chosen to work in a candle, it should burn with a bright flame. Beeswax produces a good, bright flame and a bit less soot than paraffin wax.

Heaters

A heater is anything the heats the air inside your balloon but stays on the ground after the balloon is launched. Lots of things can be used as a heater; the only requirements are that the air gets hot enough and the heater doesn't damage the balloon. All the balloons in this book can be launched with a heater instead of an onboard burner—they just won't go as far. The following are some examples of things you can use as a heater.

Blow-Dryer

This is ideal to preheat the Solar Tetroon but doesn't work so well for the other hot air balloons in this book. Blow-dryers produce a large stream of warm (not hot) air. Generally, if the air was hot enough to make your tissue paper balloon work, it would scorch the hair off your head. Most people think that would be a bad idea.

If your blow-dryer has speed and temperature settings, try the lowest speed and the highest temperature. Because the casing stays cool, you can put the nozzle of the blow-dryer right into the opening in the Solar Tetroon. Try to direct the air away from the sides, and hold the opening away from the casing of the blow-dryer to allow cooler air to escape.

Hot Air Paint Stripper or Heat Gun

This works really well for trash bag balloons and tissue paper balloons, but the casing gets too hot to work with Solar Tetroons. A heat gun is usually pistol-shaped and produces a stream of air at about 660°F (350°C). The air will quickly fill even the largest model balloon.

Be careful not to direct the air at the sides of the envelope, as it will melt polyethylene instantly and scorch through tissue paper. The metal casing gets really hot and takes a long time to cool down. Be careful where you put the heat gun down, and don't touch the casing until you are sure it is cool.

Electric Toaster

An electric toaster works very well as a heater, but it can take a long time to fill a large balloon. The air gets very hot and, as the toaster does not have a blower, it is ideal when measuring lift. Some models have casings that get very hot, so you may need to make a cardboard shield to surround the toaster.

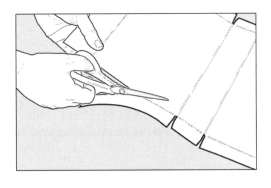

1. Open two empty cereal boxes and cut off the tabs so that you have two long cardboard strips with folds across the width.

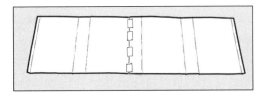

2. Join the two cereal box pieces along one of their short edges with tape so you have a very long cardboard strip folded in several places.

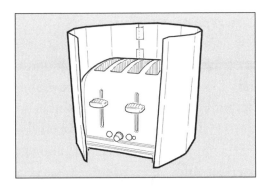

3. Wrap the cereal box strip around the electric toaster to form a shield. You may have to make more folds across the width of the strip so it curves around the toaster and cut a small notch at the bottom to let the electrical cord out. Place the gap in the strip so that you can work the controls of the toaster. If the strip is too short to go around your toaster, or if any of the metalwork of the toaster rises above the strip, you will have to make the strip larger. Set the toaster's browning control to maximum and run it empty when you are heating your balloon.

Hot Air Popcorn Maker

Some models can be adapted to heat balloons very well. If you can run the popcorn maker so the air leaving the outlet flows up into the balloon rather than sideways, the popcorn maker will fill the balloon very quickly. On some models you can remove the lid and kernel deflectors and run the popcorn maker so that the hot air is directed straight up. Most popcorn makes are only designed to run for one or two minutes at a time and need to cool down before being used again.

Camping Stove

A camping stove is very useful if you want to launch your balloon away from home. You can use gas or liquid fuel stoves, or even Sterno alcohol burners. Most camping stoves will produce plenty of hot air to fill your balloon, but you will need to protect the sides of the balloon from the flame. The best way of doing this is to use a short length of metal or ceramic pipe to make a stovepipe. You will need to find a pipe large enough to fit over your stove or at least over the burner. Cut holes in the side of the pipe near the bottom to allow air into the pipe, or rest the bottom of the stovepipe on two bricks.

If you can't find a suitable pipe, you can make a stovepipe out of wire mesh (the kind used in chicken wire) to slip over the stove. Cut a length of wire mesh and roll it into a cylinder that just slips over your stove and extends about 6 inches (15 cm) above the top. Hold it together with small wire loops. Wrap aluminum foil around the outside, leaving the bottom 1 to 2 inches (25 to 50 mm) without foil. This allows air into the bottom. Ideally, use silicone adhesive to secure the end of the foil, or you can wrap parchment/baking paper around the outside and glue the overlap with white craft glue (polyvinyl acetate, or PVA).

Launching Using a Heater

First, find a heater from the list on pages 29–32. If you are using a toaster, place it on a hard, tiled floor where it will not do any damage when it gets hot. Place a cardboard shield around the toaster (as described on page 31) and push down the lever to start the toaster working. The toaster should run empty with the color control on the darkest setting.

Open up your balloon, shaking it to fill it with cold air. Lower the balloon over the toaster and shield so that it starts to fill with hot air. Hold the balloon from the top so that the sides hang down, out of the hot air rising from the toaster slots. When the balloon starts to pull upward, just let go. (You may need to push down the toaster levers to start the heating coils again before the air is hot enough to make your balloon fly.)

If you are launching outside, you need to find a very sheltered place to put your heater. Because the balloon will fly only until the air inside cools down, you need to get the air as hot as possible. Even the slightest breeze against the balloon will start to cool the air inside.

It's a good idea to use a pair of launching poles to support your balloon while it fills. This will allow you to concentrate on keeping the sides of the balloon away from the heater flame. Push the launching poles into the ground on either side of the heater (e.g., a camping stove). Start the heater and lower the stovepipe or mesh cylinder to protect the balloon from the flame. Open up the balloon and lower it gently over the launching poles and over the heater. Keep the sides of the balloon away from the hot air rising from the stovepipe. When the balloon is pulling strongly upward, release it so it can fly away.

Launching Using an On-Board Burner

Push your launching poles into the ground 6 to 8 inches (15 to 20 cm) apart. Try to make the gap between the poles the same all the way up so the balloon can slip up and down without jamming.

Unfold your balloon and ease it over the top of the poles, making sure that the burner and its wires pass in between them. Lower it gently into place.

If you are using a liquid fuel burner, pour it slowly onto the cotton-ball burner so that it has time to soak in. Hold a plastic cup under the burner to catch any runoff. *Warning: if you let the fuel soak into the ground, it can catch on fire after you light the burner.*

Light the burner. Hold the ring at the bottom of the balloon and keep the paper away from the flame. If at any time the tissue paper catches fire, you should let go of the balloon and step away. ***Do not try to put the fire out—you will not save the balloon and you may burn yourself.***

As soon as the balloon is lifting, carefully stand up and hold up the balloon so that the burner wires clear the launch poles.

Release the balloon.

If you have a balloon that is longer than your launching poles, you can fold it in the middle where the launching poles support it. The weight of the top half will prevent the envelope from unfolding and slipping down.

Launching a Solar Tetroon

Check that the sun is strong enough using the solar power meter described earlier (page 24). If the temperature rise inside the meter is higher than 36°F (20°C), then you can launch. Fill the Solar Tetroon with warm air using a blow-dryer, hold the opening closed with one hand, and carry the tetroon outside. Rest the tetroon on the ground in full sun and wait. After a few minutes the tetroon will stir and eventually start to rise.

If there is a slight breeze, you can jump-start the Solar Tetroon. Run an extension cord from your house and into your yard so you can run a blow-dryer outside. Lay the tetroon on the ground and put your blow-dryer into the opening at the bottom. Fill the tetroon with warm air from your blow-dryer. If you have air speed and temperature settings, set the air speed to the slowest and the temperature to the highest. This will make the air as hot as possible.

The opening in the Solar Tetroon needs to be a bit bigger than the blow-dryer so there is a gap around the outside of the blow-dryer. This allows cooler air to be forced out of the tetroon and keeps air flowing through the blow-dryer. (It will overheat if no air passes through.)

Hold up the tetroon as high as possible, and when you think the tetroon is ready, let go!

The blow-dryer keeps the air inside the Solar Tetroon hot even though the breeze around the outside cools the plastic skin. As soon as you let go, the tetroon accelerates to full wind speed in a fraction of a second and the cooling effect stops. The air in the tetroon should still be hot enough to keep it flying level for a few seconds while the sun warms up the plastic skin to working temperature. Once the skin is up to temperature, you should see the Solar Tetroon start to climb.

3

The Basic Trash Bag Balloon

The Basic Trash Bag Balloon is a short cylindrical balloon about 25 inches (64 cm) high and about 20 inches (50 cm) across. The top of the balloon is closed with a straight seam, like the bottom of a tube of toothpaste. This type of seam makes two points stick out like horns on either side.

The balloon is made by cutting off the complex pleated end of a trash bag and taping the open end shut in a straight line. The straight seam increases the volume in the balloon, which increases the lift.

Thin cardboard is taped to the open edge of the balloon to keep the bottom weighed down and keep the balloon upright.

The Basic Trash Bag Balloon is very easy to make. It takes only a few minutes, has no complicated parts, and doesn't need a naked flame to make it fly.

The balloon flies well *indoors* if it is made from very thin, lightweight trash bags. The air in the balloon is heated using an electric toaster or similar electric heater, and the balloon flies until the air starts to cool. You can fly the balloon outside on still days, but you will need to run an extension cord outside for the toaster or use a different type of heater.

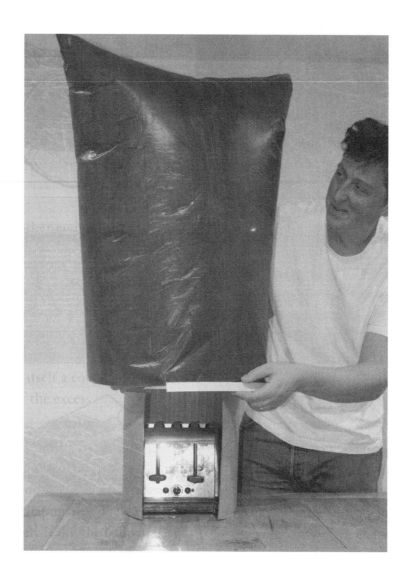

Polyethylene Balloons

A balloon is just an airtight bag full of gas. If the gas is light enough, it can lift the weight of the bag and the balloon will fly. That's it. You can make the gas bag out of pretty much anything you like, so long as it is lightweight and airtight.

Polyethylene is an ideal material for lightweight balloons. It is completely airtight and it can be made into very thin sheets that weigh almost nothing. Polyethylene is made into trash bags by blowing pressurized air into a long cylinder of hot, rubbery plastic. This makes the plastic stretch, and when it stretches it gets much thinner. If you blow a lot of air into the cylinder, you can make the plastic very thin. Ordinary trash bags use plastic sheet that is only 0.001 inch (0.02 mm) thick. That's about one-third of the thickness of a human hair.

It didn't take long for scientists to realize that polyethylene sheet is great for making balloons. Polyethylene was first produced commercially in 1939, and by 1947, giant polyethylene gas balloons were already being used in classified US military projects. For example, in 1947, Project Mogul used giant polyethylene balloons (called *Skyhook balloons*) to carry special microphones high into the stratosphere to listen for very low frequency sound waves generated by secret Soviet atomic bomb tests. By 1952, the same Skyhook balloons were carrying spy cameras over the Soviet Union to photograph research sites, military installations, and missile bases from an altitude of over 30,000 feet (9 km). Because they flew so high, Soviet warplanes could not shoot them down.

For a Basic Trash Bag Balloon, you need to use the thinnest and largest brand of trash bags you can find. Many brands of household trash bags are too thick to work well. You want the trash bags that are so thin they will split and spill garbage everywhere when you try to lift a full one! They are usually the cheapest brand; you can find some tips on finding good trash bags in chapter 11 (page 215).

Of course, you don't have to use trash bags. Any lightweight polyethylene will do. If you can find lightweight polyethylene dry cleaner bags, these work just as well. Decorating suppliers also sell thin polyethylene drop-cloth sheet to protect furniture from paint splashes. This can be taped into a cylinder to make a balloon.

Why Does Heating Air Make It Lighter?

A balloon works by having gas trapped in an airtight bag. The balloon flies when the gas is light enough to lift the bag. That's quite easy to understand when you have a lightweight gas like hydrogen or helium inside the bag, but why does hot air work? Why does air get lighter when you heat it up?

If you have a bag of gas at the same pressure as the outside world, then most of the inside of the bag will be filled with empty space. The gas is made up of solid particles called molecules, but there aren't very many of them and they are separated from each other by large distances. The space between the particles is so big that they don't have much effect on each other, and they behave like beads or marbles rattling around in the bag.

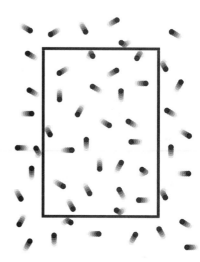

So if a bag full of gas is mostly empty space, why can't you flatten the bag so that the contents are only a few molecules thick? How do the particles of gas *know* that they have to push back when you try to squash the bag?

The answer is in all that crashing about. Any gas that is even slightly warmer than the cold depths of outer space will have atoms and molecules that zoom around. That's what heat is: the vibration or movement energy of atoms and molecules. The more energy they pick up—that is, the hotter they get—the faster they fly around inside the bag, and the

faster they crash into the walls of the bag. Molecules are very springy, so then they bounce and head off in another direction. But when the molecules crash into the wall of the bag, they give a little kick to it. Millions of molecules crash into the wall of the bag every second, each molecule giving the wall a tiny kick as it bounces off. There are so many little kicks happening that the wall feels this as a constant force spread out over its whole area. We call this spread-out force *pressure*. From this you can begin to understand how a hot air balloon gets off the ground.

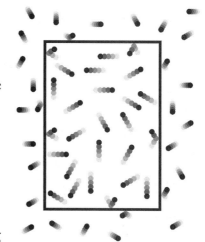

If you add heat to a gas, the molecules move around even faster. Because they are moving faster, they are going to hit the walls of the bag a lot harder and also faster—moving molecules travel across the bag in a shorter time and hit the walls more often. This means that the spread-out force on the skin of the bag will be higher—harder kicks and more of them every second. A scientist would say that the gas has a higher pressure now that it has been heated.

Gases flow from an area of high pressure to an area of low pressure. Imagine blowing out the candles on a birthday cake. You raise the pressure of the air in your lungs to make it flow out of your mouth quickly.

If you carefully make an opening in your bag of hot gas, some of the gas flows out. Because some of the gas has flowed out, the inside skin will now be getting fewer kicks than it did before. The gas will continue to flow out until the average force from the fewer but harder kicks on the inside of the bag's skin matches the force from the many more weaker kicks on the outside.

But what has happened to the gas inside the bag? The bag now contains fewer molecules than it did before we started heating the gas. The bag is the same size, but now the gas weighs less than it did before as there are fewer molecules. Scientists call the amount that a gas weighs for a given volume its *density*. So by heating the gas and allowing some of the hot gas to escape, the pressure returns to normal and you have a gas with a lower density—the gas weighs less for the same volume.

So what happens now? Imagine you hold a block of wood underwater. When you let go, the block floats up to the surface because the wood is less dense than the water surrounding it.

The balloon reacts in the same manner; it is just submerged in air rather than water. If you heat the gas inside a balloon, you make the bubble of gas inside it a lower density so that it wants to float upward, like the block in the water.

How to Make the Basic Trash Bag Balloon

Adult supervision required

Materials

Lightweight plastic trash bag
   (the thinnest you can find—
   see chapter 11, page 215)
Thin clear tape, lightweight masking tape,
   or similar
Empty cereal boxes (or other source of thin
   cardboard)

Tools

Scissors
Ruler
Pen

What to Do If Things Go Wrong

If you make small holes in the plastic sheet or there are small gaps in the seams, see chapter 11 (page 213) to find out how to fix them.

If you put the tape in the wrong place, do not try to unpeel it, as you will just tear the plastic sheet. Complete the seam as best you can and put another length of tape over the gap.

How to Make the Envelope

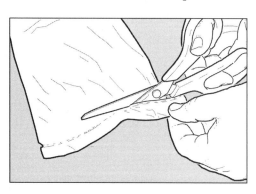

1. Carefully cut off the closed end of a plastic trash bag. Cut as close to the weld as you can. The weld is the melted line running straight across the bottom of the bag.

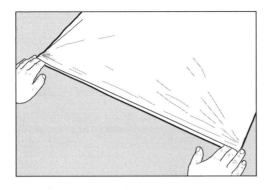

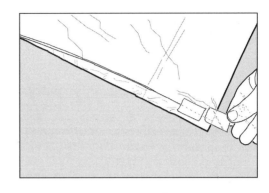

2. Open up the bag and flatten it out onto a table with one open end facing toward you.

3. Fold over ½ inch (13 mm) of the open end. Hold the folded-over edges in place with a short piece of tape, and fix the corner of the trash bag to the table with a second piece of tape.

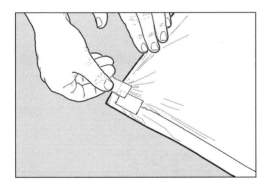

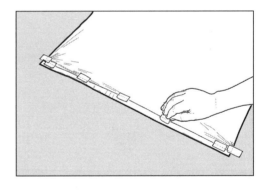

4. Pull the other side of the open end to straighten the folded-over edges and hold them in place with a short piece of tape. Attach the corner of the trash bag to the table with another piece of tape.

5. Use two or three short pieces of tape to keep the edges folded over along the entire side.

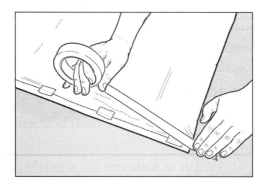

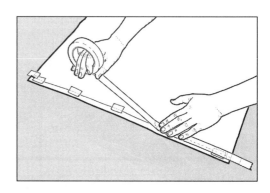

6. Affix the free end of the roll of tape to the table next to one corner of the folded-over edge. Unroll a short length of tape and line it up over the seam, but don't pull so hard that the tape stretches. Smooth the tape down onto the seam.

7. Keep the stuck-down length of tape in place with one hand and unroll another length of tape. Repeat until the whole folded-over seam is taped.

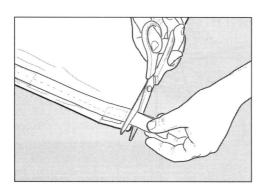

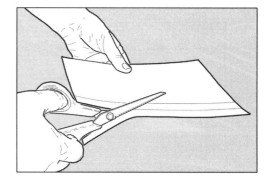

8. Lift the corner of the folded-over seam and use a pair of scissors to trim the tape close to the side of the plastic sheet. Fold any remaining stub of tape underneath the envelope.

9. Cut two strips of thin cardboard 12 inches (30 cm) long by ¾ inch (2 cm) wide from an empty cereal box or something similar.

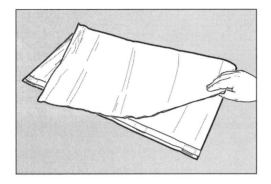 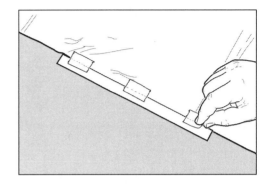

10. Turn the envelope around so that the remaining open end is toward you.

11. Attach the cardboard strips to the edge of the open end of the envelope using two or three short pieces of tape. Try to get the strips exactly opposite one another across the open end of the envelope. This will help to keep the balloon balanced.

What Next?

The balloon is complete and ready to fly. See chapter 2 for instructions on flying indoors using an electric toaster as a heater (page 33).

If lots of people are making these balloons, you can have competitions to see which balloon will stay in the air for the longest. Fly them in a large sports hall to give the balloons a chance to take off without hitting the ceiling. If you can set up a stovepipe or metal shield around a camping stove, try launching the balloons outside so you can have a competition to see which balloon will drift farthest away from the launch point. You need a fairly calm day to do this, but it can be a great way to finish a group project.

To make a Basic Trash Bag Balloon that flies even better, make an envelope from two trash bags rather than just one. Build the Trash Bag Sausage envelope described in chapter 4 (page 57), but instead of going on to make a frame and burner, just attach cardboard strips onto the bottom to keep the envelope upright.

4
The Trash Bag Sausage

The Trash Bag Sausage is a cylinder 50 inches (127 cm) tall and 20 inches (50 cm) across. The top of the balloon is closed with a straight seam like the bottom of a tube of toothpaste. This type of seam makes two points stick out like horns on either side of the balloon. The balloon is made by cutting off the ends of two trash bags and fixing them together using tape.

The bottom of the balloon is held open with a square frame made from plastic drinking straws and cardboard. Finally, there is a simple cotton-ball burner mounted on wire stretched across the frame.

To make the Trash Bag Sausage fly best, you need to find the largest and thinnest brand of bags you can. As the thinnest bags are also usually the cheapest, it is well worth searching to find a good brand. See chapter 11 (page 215) for advice on finding the right kind of trash bags. After that, if you still cannot find very thin trash bags, the "What Next?" section at the end of this chapter (page 69) will tell you how to use slightly thicker ones.

You can see the balloon for many miles at night if you use kerosene or a similar fuel that produces a luminous flame. This is because the burner is mounted at the bottom of the balloon and it can be seen without the black envelope getting in the way.

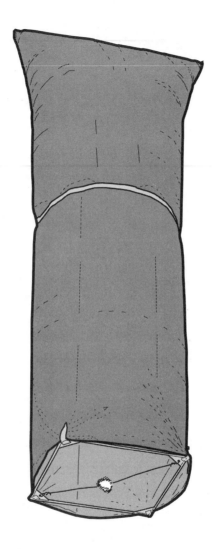

The burner is quite small for a balloon as large as this, because the air must not get too hot. If the air does get very hot, the polyethylene sheet will soften and may even melt or shrink. But because the air is only warm, there is not much lift, so the balloon must be made as light as possible. This is why it is important to use very lightweight trash bags if you can.

A Bigger Balloon Is Always Better

Somewhere in every project in this book it says that to make the balloon fly better you should make it bigger. But why does a bigger balloon fly better? And is it always the case? You might think that although a bigger envelope has more air and so more lift, it also has more weight and this would cancel out the extra lift.

In fact, bigger balloons have a lot more lift, much more than the extra weight of a bigger envelope. This is because the volume of a three-dimensional shape grows faster than its surface area as the shape gets bigger. Because the lift depends on the volume of the shape, and the weight depends on the surface area, more lift is left over as the shape gets bigger. The best way to understand how this works is to look at an example.

Imagine you have two hot air balloons each shaped like a cube. One balloon has sides that are 1 meter along each edge, and the other has sides that are 2 meters along each edge. Both balloons have four tissue paper sides and a top, with the bottom face left open to allow the hot air in.

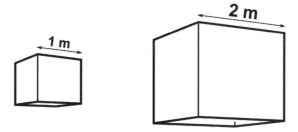

If you want to calculate the volume of each balloon, multiply the width by the depth by the height. As they are both cubes, this is easy.

The volume for the smaller balloon is $1 \times 1 \times 1 = \textbf{1 m}^3$.

The volume for the larger balloon is $2 \times 2 \times 2 = \textbf{8 m}^3$.

So the volume has increased eight times by making the sides twice as long. How much has the *weight* of the envelope increased?

The weight of the balloon is made up of the weight of paper needed to make a cube-shaped envelope.

That is just the area of paper you need to make five square faces multiplied by how much the paper weighs per square meter. (Assume each square meter of tissue paper weighs about 15 grams.) The area of a square face is easy to work out—you multiply the width by the height:

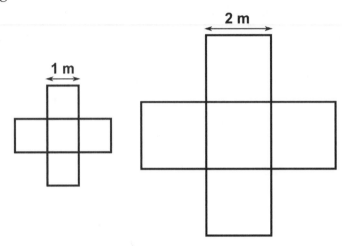

For the smaller balloon, the area of one side is 1 × 1 = 1 m².
The area for five square faces is 5 × 1 = 5 m².
So the smaller envelope weighs 15 × 5 = **75 grams.**
For the larger balloon, the area of one side is 2 × 2 = 4 m².
The area for five square faces is 5 × 4 = 20 m².
So the larger envelope weighs 15 × 20 = **300 grams.**

Overall, this means that the volume of the larger balloon is *eight times* that of the smaller balloon, and so it has eight times the lift. The weight of the larger balloon is only *four times* bigger than the weight of the smaller balloon. Since the larger balloon has eight times the lift, it's no surprise that the larger balloon flies better!

But things get even more interesting if we look at the lift available to carry a payload at the end of a flight as the burner flame gets smaller. If the air inside both balloons is heated to only 30°C above the surrounding air:

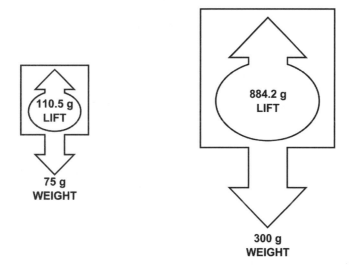

Smaller balloon lift from the heated air = 110.5 grams
Lift available for payload = lift − envelope weight = 110.5 − 75 = ***35.5 grams***
Larger balloon lift from the heated air = 884.2 grams
Lift available for payload = 884.2 − 300 = ***584.2 grams***

So the larger balloon can lift a payload that is more than *16 times* bigger. This means that the larger balloon will continue flying well even as the burner starts to run out.

If you make balloons bigger, they fly better. But what happens if you make a smaller balloon? Obviously they don't fly as well because they have less lift. In fact, if you make a tissue paper balloon too small, it won't fly at all.

How to Make the Trash Bag Sausage

Adult supervision required

Materials

2 lightweight plastic trash bags (the thinnest you can find—see chapter 11, page 215)

Thin clear tape, lightweight masking tape, or similar, ¾ or 1 inch (19 mm or 25 mm) wide

14 jumbo plastic drinking straws, ¼-inch (6 mm) diameter

Empty cereal boxes (or other source of thin cardboard)

Thin, soft, iron wire

Cotton ball, about 2 inches (5 cm) in diameter

1 fluid ounce (30 mL) kerosene

Tools

Scissors

Ruler

2-inch (5 cm) ball of modeling clay

Pencil

Straight (dressmaker's) pin

Pliers (with wire cutters)

Lighter or matches

What to Do If Things Go Wrong

If you make small holes in the plastic sheet or there are small gaps in the seams, see chapter 11 (page 213) to find out how to fix them.

If you put the tape in the wrong place, do not try to unpeel it, as you will just tear the plastic sheet. Complete the seam as best you can and put another length of tape over the gap.

How to Make the Envelope

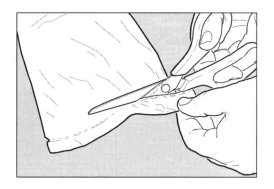

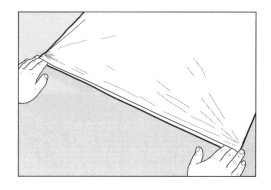

1. Carefully cut the closed end off a plastic trash bag. Cut as close to the weld as you can. The weld is the melted line running straight across the bottom of the bag.

2. Open up the bag and flatten it out onto a table with one open end facing toward you.

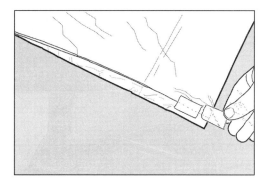

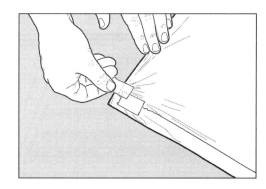

3. Fold over ½ inch (13 mm) of the open end. Hold the folded-over edges in place with a short piece of tape, and secure the corner of the trash bag to the table with a second piece of tape.

4. Pull the other side of the open end to straighten the folded-over edges and hold them in place with a short piece of tape. Attach the corner of the trash bag to the table with another piece of tape.

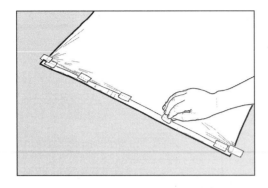

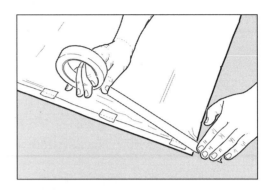

5. Use two or three short pieces of tape to keep the edges folded over along the entire side.

6. Affix the free end of the roll of tape to the table next to one corner of the folded-over edge. Unroll a short length of tape and line it up over the seam, but don't pull so hard that the tape stretches. Smooth the tape down onto the seam.

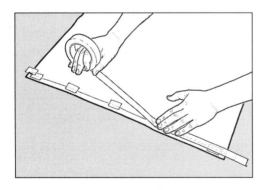

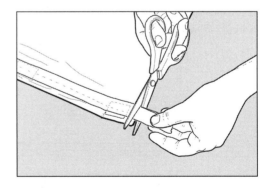

7. Keep the stuck-down length of tape in place with one hand and unroll another length of tape. Repeat until the whole folded-over seam is taped.

8. Lift the corner of the folded-over seam and cut the tape close to the side of the envelope with a pair of scissors. Fold any remaining stub of tape underneath the envelope.

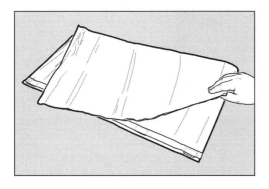

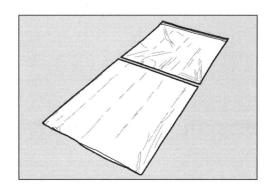

9. Turn the envelope around so that the remaining open end is toward you.

10. Take a second trash bag and flatten it out with one of the open ends next to the open end of the envelope.

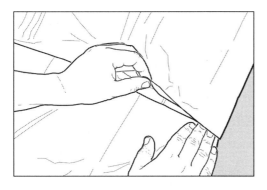

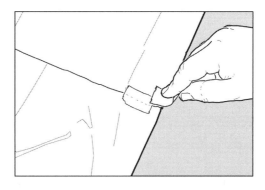

11. Slide the new trash bag into the open end of the envelope and position it so that there is a ½-inch (13 mm) overlap all the way along the edge.

12. Place a short length of tape across the seam to keep the two bags together and use a second short piece of tape to hold the end of the seam to the table.

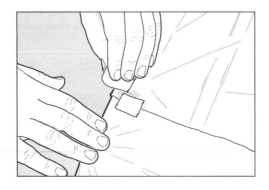

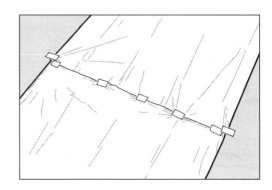

13. Pull the other end of the seam to straighten it. Check that the overlap is still ½ inch (13 mm) all the way along the side and secure the end of the seam with two short pieces of tape as you did in the previous step.

14. Put three more small pieces of tape along the seam, making sure that the overlap is ½ inch (13 mm) all the way along the side.

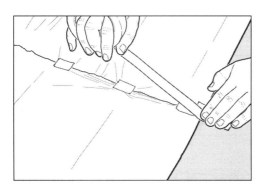

15. Affix the free end of the roll of tape to the table next to one side of the seam. Unroll a length of tape, line it up over the seam, and smooth it down.

16. Keep the stuck-down length of tape in place with one hand and unroll another length of tape. Smooth the tape down over the seam. Repeat until the whole folded-over seam is taped over.

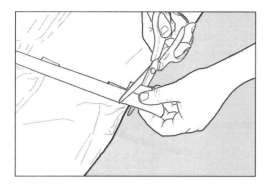

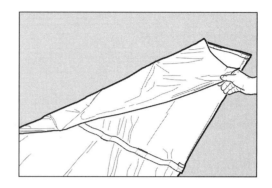

17. Lift the ends of the seam and cut the tape close to the side of the envelope with a pair of scissors. Fold any remaining stub of tape under the envelope.

18. Turn the envelope over and lay it down, carefully flattening out the seam so that the taped part lies flat on the table.

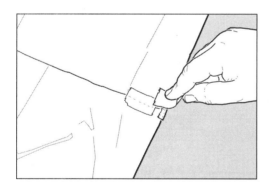

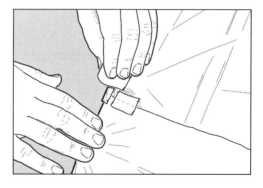

19. Check that the overlap is still ½ inch (13 mm) all the way along the side. Place a short length of tape across the seam at one end and use a second piece of tape to hold the end of the seam down to the table.

20. Pull the other end of the seam to straighten it. Check that the overlap is still ½ inch (13 mm) all the way along the side and secure the end of the seam with two short pieces of tape as you did in the previous step.

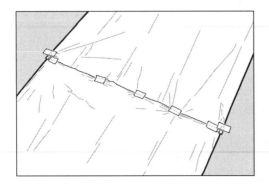

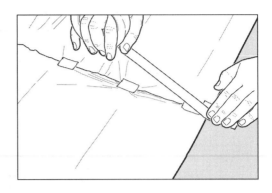

21. Put three more small pieces of tape along the seam, making sure that the overlap is ½ inch (13 mm) all the way along.

22. Affix the free end of the roll of tape to the table next to one side of the seam. Unroll a length of tape, line it up over the seam, and smooth it down.

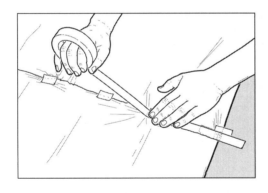

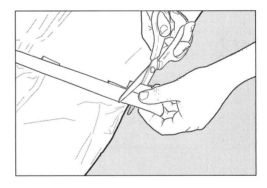

23. Keep the stuck-down length of tape in place with one hand and unroll another length of tape. Smooth the tape down over the seam. Repeat until the whole folded-over seam is taped.

24. Lift the ends of the seam and trim the tape with a pair of scissors. Fold any remaining stub of tape under the envelope.

How to Make the Drinking Straw Frame

25. Lay the completed envelope flat on the table and measure across the opening at the bottom. You will need four plastic drinking straws exactly half the length measured in this step. This means you have to join two or three ordinary straws together to make a long straw.

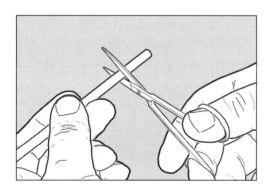

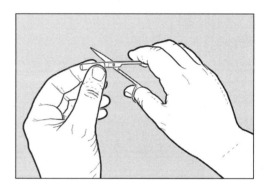

26. Cut a sleeve 1 inch (25 mm) long from a spare straw.

27. Cut the sleeve along its length.

28. Slip two straws into this sleeve. Make sure both straws are pushed all the way into the middle so they touch.

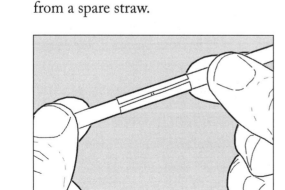

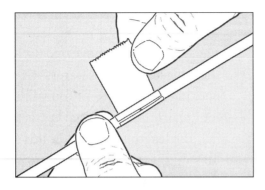

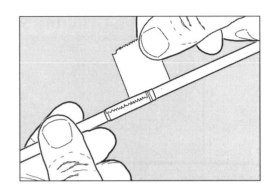

29. Hold the sleeve tight and wrap a small piece of tape across the cut in the sleeve.

30. Put tape around the seams between the sleeve and straws. Join this double-length straw to another ordinary straw in the same way to make a triple-length straw. Make four of these long straws.

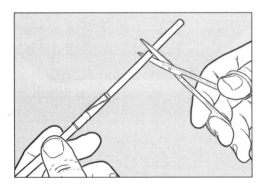

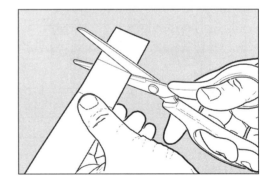

30. Cut the long straws so they are *exactly half* the length you measured in step 25.

32. Cut out two 1½-inch (38 mm) squares of thin cardboard from an empty cereal box or something similar.

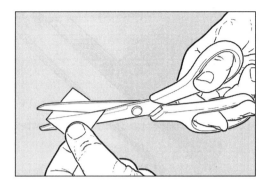

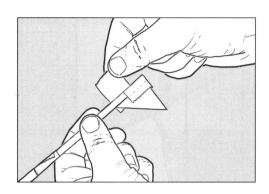

33. Cut both squares across a diagonal line so that you have four right-angled triangles.

34. Use two short pieces of tape to attach one of the triangles to the end of one of the long straws as shown.

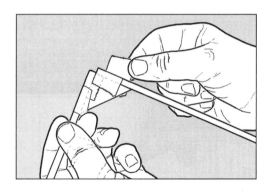

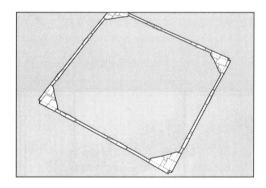

35. Attach a second straw to the other side of the cardboard triangle as shown.

36. Join all of the straws together using the cardboard triangles and tape to form a square frame.

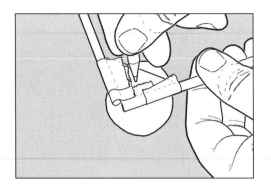

37. Put one of the cardboard triangles on top of a piece of modeling clay and push a sharp pencil through the middle of the triangle to make a small hole (about ⅛ inch or 3 mm across). Make a second hole through the card triangle in the far corner (across the diagonal of the square frame).

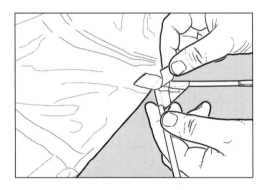

38. Attach a corner of the frame to the open edge of the envelope using tape.

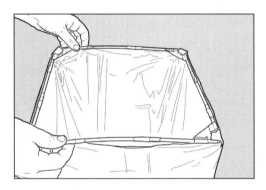

39. Repeat so that all four corners of the frame are attached to the envelope.

How to Make a Cotton-Ball Burner

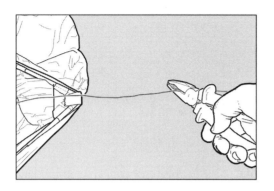

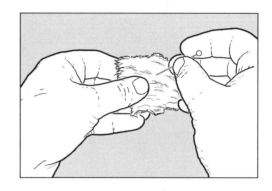

40. Stretch a piece of wire diagonally across the frame. Cut the wire so that it is 6 inches (15 cm) longer than the distance across the corners of the frame.

41. Push a straight pin through a 2-inch (5 cm) cotton ball to make a hole.

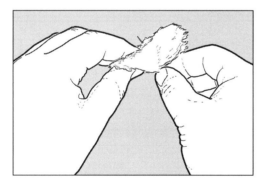

42. Grip the cotton ball at least ½ inch (13 mm) away from the pin and gently pull the pin sideways to enlarge the hole. If you grip the cotton ball too close to the pin, the cotton fibers won't slide over each other and the pin won't move.

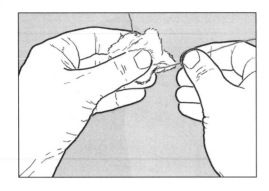

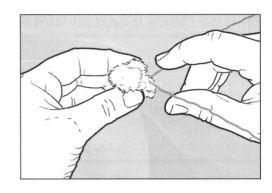

43. Feed the wire through the hole in the cotton ball. When the ball is in the middle, bend the wire in half, leaving the cotton ball on the bend.

44. Twist the wire together a few times close to the cotton ball.

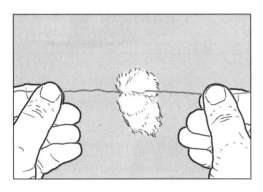

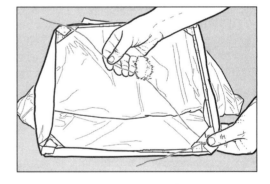

45. Stretch out the wires on either side as shown.

46. Push one of the burner wires through the hole in the one of the cardboard triangles. Position the cotton ball in the middle of the frame and fold the burner wire down over the card triangle. Twist the end of the burner wire around itself a couple of times and cut off the excess.

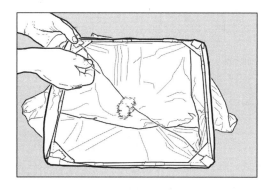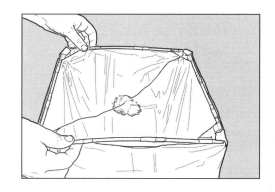

47. Push the other burner wire through the cardboard triangle on the opposite side of the frame. Straighten the burner wire and make sure the frame is still square. Bend the second burner wire down over the card triangle, fold the burner wire around itself a couple of times, and cut off the excess.

48. The completed burner is in place.

What Next?

Check the envelope for any leaks by inflating it over an electric toaster or similar heater (see page 29). Take care not to scorch the cotton-ball burner or melt either the polyethylene envelope or the drinking straws. Look for gaps in the seams and repair them using small pieces of tape.

Once you have fixed any leaks, the balloon is complete and ready to fly. See chapter 2 (page 33) for instructions on flying a balloon with a burner.

If you can only find regular-thickness trash bags, you can get the Trash Bag Sausage to work if you use three trash bags to make the envelope rather than two. Complete the envelope as shown in this chapter but then repeat steps 10 to 24 to add the third trash bag. Then, continue on to add the base frame and burner. This larger balloon takes a while to fill and is still a bit heavy for the burner size, but it should fly.

Of course, if you do have very thin trash bags, an envelope made from three very thin trash bags will fly even better!

5
The Kongming Lantern

The Kongming Lantern has a unique tapered shape that has a square cross-section at the top and a round cross-section at the bottom. The design in this book is about 48 inches (120 cm) tall and 24 inches (60 cm) wide at the top.

The balloon envelope is made from tissue paper glued together with diluted white craft glue (PVA glue). The tissue paper panels making the envelope are joined together with a "fin seam" that sticks out from the surface of the envelope. This type of seam is very easy to form and, more important, is very easy to make airtight. Leaks allow the hot air to escape, and the balloon will not fly as well.

There is a ring made from thin iron wire fixed into the opening at the bottom of the envelope. A simple cotton-ball burner is fixed into the middle of a thin wire stretched across the middle of the base ring.

The Kongming Lantern is one of the easiest tissue paper balloons to make, because it has simple, straight seams and is made from only four panels. As it has such a simple envelope and also uses a simple burner, the Kongming Lantern is a good design to choose for your first tissue paper balloon.

As the name suggests, Kongming lanterns are usually released at night. Because of the thin tissue paper used to make them, the whole envelope glows brightly when they fly. Kongming lanterns are released in large numbers during the Chinese Autumn Festival. Many people write their hopes for the new year onto the paper envelope before they release their balloon.

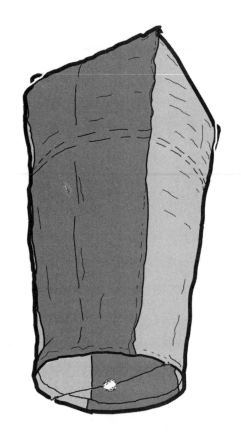

If you want to launch a balloon at night, you need to have a bright luminous flame in your burner. The color of the flame depends on the type of fuel you use and how well it burns. Kerosene and diesel fuel are good for night launches, as they burn with a bright yellow flame. Unfortunately, the flame also produces a great deal of soot, so the envelope usually lasts for only a couple of flights as it gets so caked with soot.

Why Does a Balloon Full of Light Gas Rise?

You've probably heard the simple explanation that a balloon rises because the gas inside is lighter than the surrounding air. But why should a bubble of gas rise just because it is lighter than the air around it?

Imagine you have two cube-shaped build-ing blocks, both the same size, on a table in front of you. One is made from a light wood, such as pine or balsa, and the other darker block is made of metal.

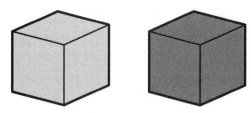

Both blocks press down on the table beneath them, but obviously the metal block presses down harder because it is heavier. The weight is spread out over the area of the bottom of the block, and we call a force spread out over an area *pressure*. The pressure under the metal block is higher, even though the area in contact with the table is the same for each block.

Now imagine that you put four more metal blocks on top of both blocks to make a square column.

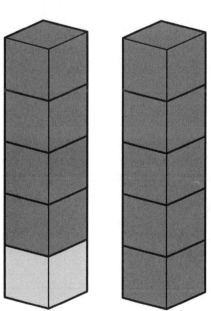

Now the pressure has increased under both blocks. But the pressure under the wooden block is still a bit less than the pressure under the metal block, because the weight of the five metal blocks is more than the weight of the wooden block plus four metal blocks.

Take the wooden block and put it under the surface of the water in a fish tank.

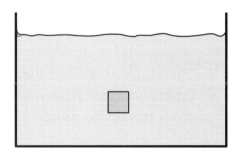

A cube of water doesn't weigh as much as a cube of metal, but it is still heavier than the cube of light wood. So in the tank you get something just like the stack of blocks on the table. Imagine two square columns next to one another made of water. They don't flow out sideways because there is more water all around them, but gravity still makes the water press down.

The pressure under each column depends on the weight of the whole square column. The light wood weighs less than the same amount of water, so the pressure under the all-water column is higher than the pressure under the column with a wooden block at the bottom. Of course, there are identical all-water columns surrounding the wooden block. Because the surrounding water pressure pushes up against the bottom face of the block harder than the block itself is pushing down, the result is that the block is forced up.

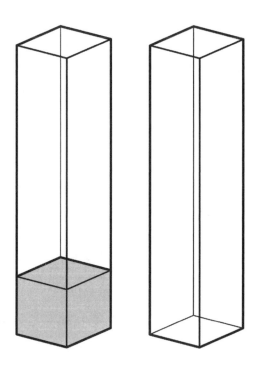

It may seem that this explanation has moved a long way away from balloons, but the air behaves in the same way as water in a tank or pool. In fact, you could say that we live at the bottom of a swimming pool of air that covers all of the Earth. Of course, the pool is about 60 miles (100 km) deep!

Because air pressure works the same way as water pressure, a lightweight balloon of hot air receives an upward push in the same way as the block in the pool. The balloon is lighter than the same volume of air, so the pressure on the bottom of the balloon is a little less than atmospheric pressure. The air pressure pushes the bottom of the balloon up.

How to Make the Kongming Lantern

Adult supervision required

Materials

8 sheets of tissue paper, 20 inches by 26 inches (50 cm by 66 cm) or larger

1 cup (240 mL) diluted white craft glue (1 part PVA glue to 5 parts water)

6½ feet (2 m) thin, soft iron wire

Cotton ball, about 2 inches (5 cm) in diameter

1 fluid ounce (30 mL) kerosene

Tools

Narrow sponge or brush (to apply glue)

6 straight (dressmaker's) pins

Ruler

Pen

Scissors

Long, straight-edge plank of wood or similar

Heavy books or food cans to hold down the tissue paper

Clean sponge and dry cloth

Pliers (with wire cutters)

8 paper clips

8 cardboard rectangles, 2 inches (5 cm) long by ¾ inch (2 cm) wide, folded in half

Before You Start

You will need a large, flat surface to build your balloon. You can use a table or the floor, but whatever you use is going to get glue on it, so make sure the glue won't damage it. You can help to protect the table or floor by cutting trash bags into large plastic sheets to cover the work area.

If you do cover your table with plastic sheets, you can leave the balloon on the table to dry, as white craft glue will not stick to the plastic used to make trash bags. The balloon will dry more slowly if you leave it on the table rather than hang it up, but it is a lot easier.

As with any tissue paper balloon, it is a good idea to **have the bottom 12 inches (30 cm) of the balloon coated with a fire retardant.** You need to coat the tissue paper before you create the balloon—see chapter 11 (page 221) for instructions.

When you make a tissue paper balloon, most of your time is spent waiting for the glue to dry. If you have a blow-dryer, you can make a balloon much more quickly by using the blow-dryer to blow warm air at the glued seams. ***Don't use a fan heater or other room heater as they can set the tissue paper on fire.***

What to Do If Things Go Wrong

Holes in tissue paper are easy to fix, and a repaired Kongming Lantern will still fly well. You can find instructions for repairing holes in chapter 11 (page 211).

In fact, check chapter 11 if you have accidentally glued parts of the panels that shouldn't be glued together, if you need a recipe for a different glue, if you cannot find the right materials, or if you have any other problems.

How to Make the Envelope

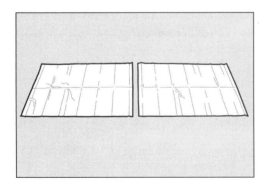

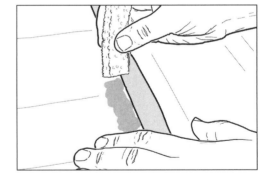

1. Put two tissue paper sheets on a large table or on the floor. Arrange them so they meet along their narrow edges.

2. Wet a narrow sponge (or brush) with diluted glue and squeeze it out so that it is nearly dry. Apply glue to the edge of the left-hand sheet of tissue paper.

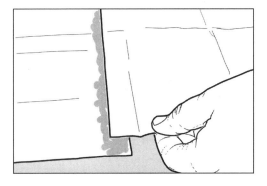

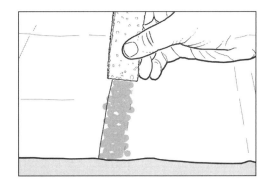

3. Lift the right-hand sheet of tissue paper, line it up over the glued edge, and press down.

4. Apply more glue to the seam so that it soaks through both sheets. This will glue together any dry patches.

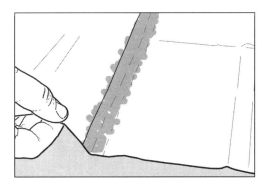

5. Gently lift the left-hand sheet of tissue paper so that both sheets peel away from the table or floor. Put the pair of tissue paper sheets over the back of a chair or over a door so that they can dry. Repeat these steps until you have four panels made from pairs of tissue paper sheets.

6. After the panels have dried completely, lay all four of them in a stack on the table or floor. Smooth the panels down and carefully line up their top and left-hand edges. Use straight pins to hold the panels together along both long edges.

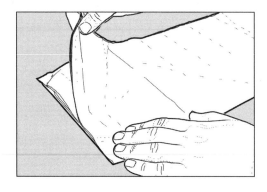

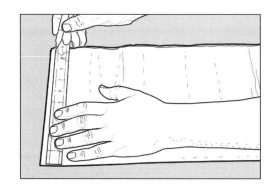

7. Fold the whole stack in half so that the long edges meet and the fold is toward you.

8. Measure the width of the left-hand end of the stack. If the panels don't quite line up, then measure to the narrowest panel.

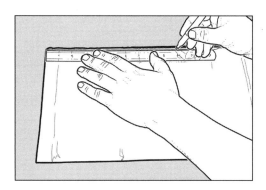

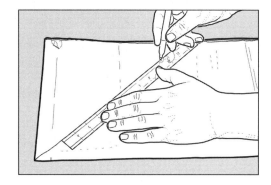

9. Measure the same length along the far edge of the stack and make a mark. If the edges of the panels don't line up properly, then make the mark on the narrowest panel.

10. Draw a line connecting the left-hand corner of the fold to the mark you made in step 9.

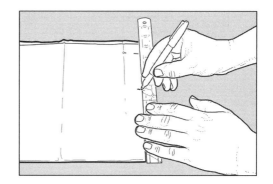

11. Cutting off as little paper as possible, trim the right-hand end of the stack of panels so that they are all the same length.

12. Measure 6 inches (15 cm) up from the fold and make a mark on the right-hand edge of the stack of panels.

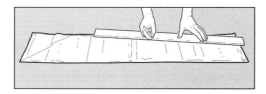

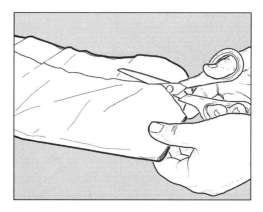

13. Draw a line from this mark to the end of the diagonal line that you drew in step 10. You will need to use either a long ruler or the edge of a plank of wood, as shown. Ideally the ruler or plank should be long enough to draw the entire line at once.

14. Cut along the two lines. Keep the panels lined up while you cut.

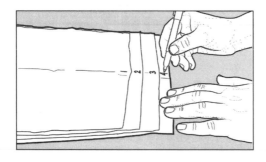

15. Open out the panels and write a number at the bottom end of each panel. The pointed end will be the top and the flat end will be the bottom. Remember to number alternating color panels if you are making a two-colored Kongming Lantern.

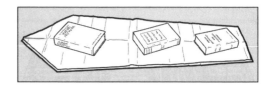

16. Lay panel 1 on the table or floor with the pointed end (top end) on your left-hand side. Lay panel 2 on top and slide it away from you by ½ inch (13 mm) to expose a strip of panel 1 along the near side. Check that the exposed strip is even along its length and then put a few heavy books or food cans on top to keep both panels from moving.

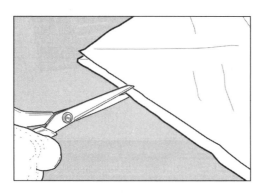

17. Make a series of cuts spaced 4 inches (10 cm) apart across the projecting strip of the lower panel. Make sure that you only cut across the projecting strip and not into the upper panel.

18. Wet the sponge with diluted glue and squeeze it out so that it is nearly dry. Dab the sponge along the edge of the top panel to make a strip about ½ inch (13 mm) wide, wet with glue.

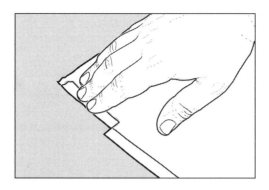

19. Fold the flap up onto the glued strip of the upper panel and pat it down.

20. Dab the sponge over the flap to stick down any dry patches. Continue with the rest of the flaps until you finish the seam. Peel the envelope off the table or floor and hang it over the back of a chair to dry. Wipe the glue off the work area with a clean sponge and dry with a cloth.

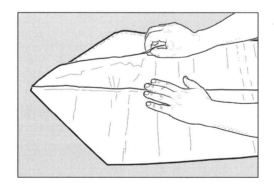

21. When the seam is dry, put the envelope back on the table or floor with panel 2 on the bottom. Make sure that the pointed end (the top of the envelope) is still on your left-hand side. Fold back the top panel (panel 1) so that the free edges line up with the seam at the back of the envelope. Make a neat crease down the middle. This puts panel 1 safely out of the way and leaves panel 2 exposed so it is easy to join to panel 3.

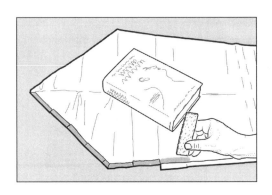

22. Lay panel 3 on top of the envelope. Slide panel 3 away from you by ½ inch (13 mm) to expose a strip of the lower panel—just as you did in step 16. Once you are sure that the exposed strip of the lower panel is even along its length, put some heavy books or food cans on top to keep everything lined up.

23. Make the seam just as you did in steps 17 to 20. Peel the envelope off the table or floor and hang over a chair to dry. Clean and dry the work area.

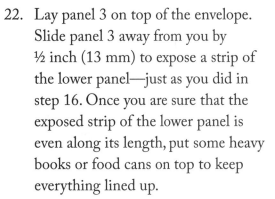

24. When the seam is dry, put the envelope back on the table or floor with panel 3 on the bottom. Make sure that the pointed end is still on the left. Carefully fold back all of the panels except the bottom one (panel 3). Line up the edges of the panels with the seam at the back of the lowest panel and form a crease. Now all of the panels should sit out of the way, leaving panel 3 exposed at the bottom.

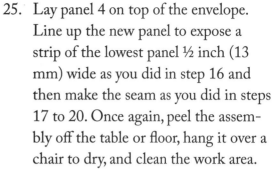

25. Lay panel 4 on top of the envelope. Line up the new panel to expose a strip of the lowest panel ½ inch (13 mm) wide as you did in step 16 and then make the seam as you did in steps 17 to 20. Once again, peel the assembly off the table or floor, hang it over a chair to dry, and clean the work area.

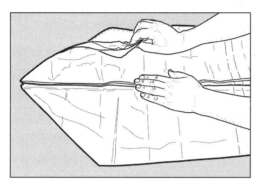

26. When the seam is dry, put the envelope back on the table or floor with panel 4 on the bottom. Make sure that the pointed end is on your left-hand side. Carefully fold back all of the panels except the bottom one (panel 4). Line up the edges of the panels with the seam at the back of the bottom panel and form a crease so that they sit in a stack neatly out of the way.

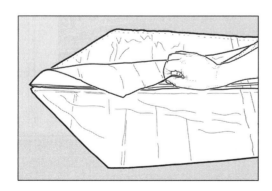

27. Take the edge of the top panel on the stack (panel 1) and fold it forward again over the bottom panel (panel 4). Line up the top panel to expose a ½-inch (13 mm) strip of the bottom panel as you did before. This will be more difficult than before as the back edge of the top panel is already joined to the envelope. Use heavy books or food cans to hold the top panel in place.

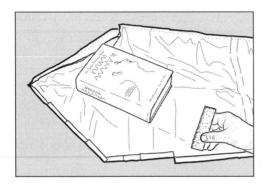

28. Form the seam as you did in steps 17 to 20. Peel the envelope off the table or floor, hang it up to dry, and clean the work area.

How to Fit a Thin Wire Ring

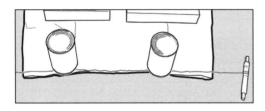

29. Open up the envelope and then flatten it down on the table or floor so the seams run down the middle of the envelope and not at the sides. Stretch a wire along the base of the balloon and hold it in place with a couple of food cans. The wire should overhang both sides by at least 2 inches (5 cm).

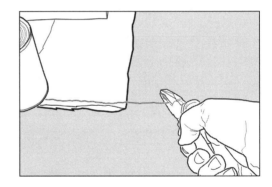

30. Cut the wire 2 inches (5 cm) from the side of the balloon. Repeat so that you have two wires laid along the base of the balloon.

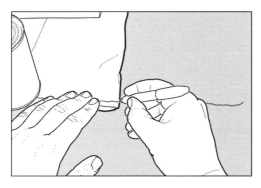

31. Mark both wires where they cross the side of the balloon. Repeat on the other side of the balloon.

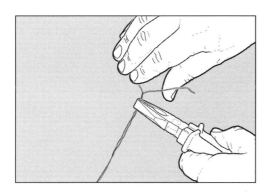

32. Use a pair of pliers to grip both of the wires next to the marks. Twist the short ends together so that the twist starts at the marks. Once the twist is about ½ inch (13 mm) long, cut off the rest of the short ends next to the twist. Repeat with the marks at the other end of the wires.

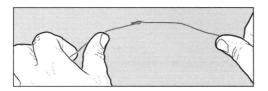

33. Open the wire into a ring. Bend the wires to get the curve of the ring as even as possible. Bend the twists to lie against the side of the ring. Open up the bottom of the balloon and put the ring inside.

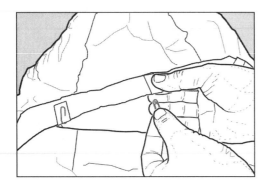

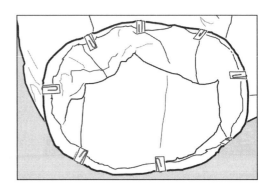

34. Take ½ inch (13 mm) of the bottom edge of the balloon opening and fold it over the wire ring. Hold the tissue paper over the wire ring by folding a small piece of cardboard over the edge and securing it with a paper clip.

35. Repeat this process so that there are eight paper clips all around the opening. Lay the balloon flat on the table or floor with the ring on top. Draw the lower edge toward you to ensure that none of the envelope is trapped underneath.

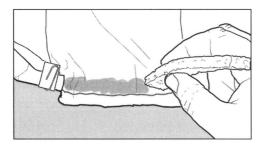

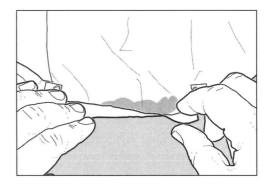

36. Tear the lower edge of the balloon between two of the cardboard strips to form a flap. Fold the flap down onto the table or floor and glue the tissue paper above the wire as shown. Make sure that the glue doesn't stick the tissue paper to the cardboard strip.

37. Fold the flap back up and pat onto the wet tissue paper.

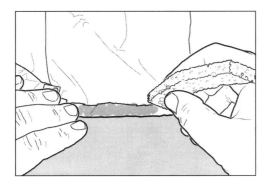

38. Rewet the flap to stick down any dry patches. Lift the balloon off the table or floor and clean the glue from the work area.

    Because the tissue paper gets very weak when it is wet, you should only glue alternate gaps between the cardboard strips. You can glue the rest after the first gaps are dry.

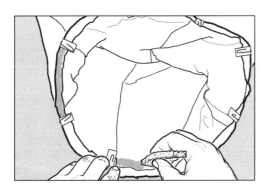

39. Lift the balloon up, turn it so that the next-but-one gap is toward you, and lay the balloon down onto the table or floor. Tear down a flap and glue it as before. Lift the balloon up carefully, and clean the glue from the work area.

    Repeat these steps until you have glued half of the gaps. Put the balloon to one side and prop the base ring up until the glued flaps are dry. Remove all of the cardboard strips. Hold the balloon up and rotate it until one of the loose flaps is toward you. Lay the balloon on the table or floor and draw the near edge of the base ring toward you to ensure that none of the envelope is trapped underneath.

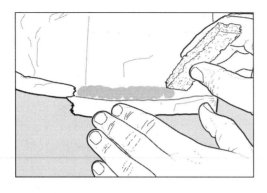

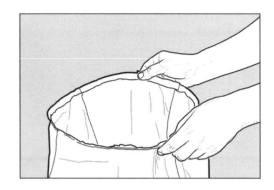

40. Glue the remaining flaps in the same way and put the completed balloon to one side to dry.

41. Now you have a completed base ring.

How to Make a Cotton-Ball Burner

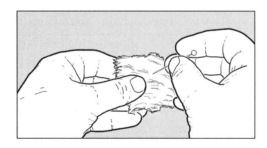

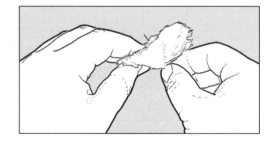

42. Use a straight pin to force a hole through a cotton ball.

43. Grip the cotton ball at least ½ inch (13 mm) away from the pin and gently pull the pin sideways to enlarge the hole. (If you grip too close, the pin will not move.) Lay a piece of wire across the opening at the bottom of the envelope. Cut the wire so it is 6 inches (15 cm) longer than the distance across the opening.

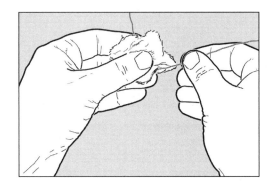

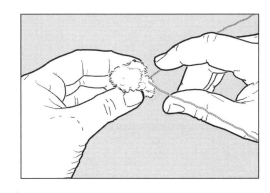

44. Push the wire through the hole in the cotton ball. When the ball is in the middle, bend the wire in half, leaving the cotton ball on the bend.

45. Twist the wire together a few times close to the cotton ball.

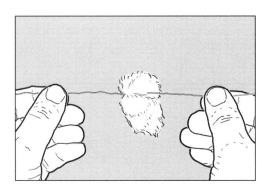

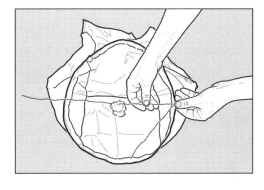

46. Stretch out the wires on either side as shown.

47. Push one of the burner wires through the tissue paper just above the base ring wire. Position the cotton ball in the center of the circle and fold the burner wire down over the base ring wire. Twist the end of the burner wire around itself a couple of times and cut off the excess.

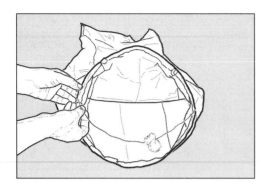 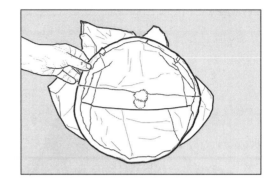

48. Push the other end of the burner wire through the tissue paper on the opposite side of the base ring. Straighten the burner wire and make sure the base ring is circular. Bend the second burner wire down over the base ring wire, fold the burner wire around on itself a couple of times, and cut off the excess.

49. The completed burner is in place.

What Next?

Check the envelope for any leaks by inflating it over an electric toaster or similar heater (see page 29). Look for gaps in the seams or holes in the tissue paper and repair them (see instructions in chapter 11, page 211). Take care not to scorch the cotton-ball burner. Once you have fixed any leaks, the balloon is complete and ready to fly. See chapter 2 (page 33) for instructions on flying a balloon with a burner.

Applying a fire retardant to the tissue paper will almost completely eliminate burn-ups on launching. If the wind catches the burner flame and pushes it onto the side of the envelope, all that will happen is the flame will scorch a hole through the tissue paper.

Be aware that grazing animals will often try to eat a crashed balloon and may be injured if wire has been used to make it. If you live in an area that contains a lot of livestock, you can make a Kongming Lantern with a wire-free burner. Make the envelope as described in this chapter (steps 1 to 28) and follow the instructions to fit the wire-free burner from chapter 6 (step 35 onward). Because the Kongming Lantern has less lift than the Montgolfiere, you will need to use ⅛-inch-by-³⁄₁₆-inch (3 mm by 5 mm) balsa wood sticks instead of ¼-inch (6 mm) hardwood dowels. (If you can find a dowel smaller than ¼ inch, this might work as well.)

A Traditional-Shape Kongming Lantern

If you want to make a larger, more traditionally shaped Kongming Lantern, start by gluing three sheets of 24-inch-by-20-inch (60 cm by 50 cm) tissue paper together along their long edges as shown.

Make four panels like this and follow the instructions in this chapter from steps 6 to 28 to make the envelope.

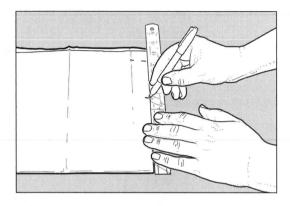

In step 12 you should measure 8 inches (20 cm) up from the fold rather than 6 inches (15 cm) so the opening is a bit bigger.

This Kongming Lantern will need a heavier ring than the one described in this chapter to keep it upright. Use a rattan ring (chapter 7) or a simple thick wire ring (chapter 8). You can fit any burner from the other chapters, but the waxed string burner (chapter 7) is the closest one to a traditional Kongming Lantern burner.

6
The Montgolfiere

The Montgolfiere balloon has a classic modern hot air balloon shape—an upside-down teardrop. It is about 48 inches (120 cm) tall by 32 inches (80 cm) across and made from six flat panels of tissue paper cut so that when they are glued together, the balloon has an elegant curved shape.

The balloon has a wooden frame glued into the opening at the bottom and a burner made from aluminum foil and a cotton ball. No wire is used in this balloon, so it is a good balloon to make if you live in an area with a lot of livestock that could injure themselves by eating the wire in a crashed balloon.

Any thin wood can be used to make the wooden frame: 3/16-inch (5 mm) square balsa makes a very light but fragile frame; a 1/4-inch (6 mm) hardwood dowel makes a heavier and much stronger frame. Both fly well.

Because the balloon is made with six panels rather than four, the envelope has a bigger diameter than the other tissue paper balloons in this book and holds a lot of air. This gives the balloon a lot of lift, even though it is not very tall.

The shape of the balloon is based on the designs of the French Montgolfier brothers, who flew the first manned hot air balloon in 1783, and on the designs of the American Ed Yost, who developed the first modern hot air balloon in 1955.

Balloon Shapes

The balloon in this chapter is called the Montgolfiere because of its teardrop shape, but in the world of balloons the term *Montgolfiere* has nothing to do with a balloon's shape. A Montgolfiere is a balloon that uses only hot air to keep it flying, so technically all of the balloons in this book are Montgolfieres. Most full-size hot air balloons are Montgolfieres, because it is the cheapest and safest form of balloon. Some long-distance balloons, called *Roziers*, have special chambers built into the envelope to hold helium gas as well as the hot air, but these are much more expensive to build and more difficult to fly.

From Jacques Charles's balloon in 1783 until Ed Yost's modern hot air balloon in 1955, almost all free-flying balloons were made with spherical envelopes filled with hydrogen. A sphere uses the smallest amount of fabric for a given volume, so the envelope will be lighter and the lift will be greater. The only thing you need to do with a gas balloon is let out a little bit of gas so the balloon doesn't fly too high and burst, and let out a bit more when you want the balloon to come down. But to keep a hot air balloon flying, you must keep feeding hot air into the envelope to replace the air inside as it cools—there needs to be a hole in the bottom of the envelope for the hot air to enter. Because of this, the most efficient shape for a hot air balloon is an upside-down teardrop, and almost all full-size hot air balloons have been made this way.

Hot air balloons can be made in a lot of different shapes, and if you go to a hot air balloon festival you will see balloons shaped like cartoon characters, beer bottles, and animals. But these special balloons are more difficult to fly and use a lot more fuel to keep them flying. The best shape is the simple upside-down teardrop.

Because of its tapered shape, the Montgolfiere is also a very stable balloon and will right itself quickly if a gust of wind tips it up. But why does the shape make a difference?

Why Doesn't a Hot Air Balloon Turn Upside Down?

Along with having plenty of lift and a good, airtight, lightweight envelope, one of the most important things about a model balloon is how it behaves in windy weather. Often a gust of wind will catch a balloon just after it has launched and tilt it on its side. If the balloon tilts too easily, it will lose hot air, and if it takes too long to right itself, then the burner flame could set the envelope on fire.

So what makes a balloon sit back upright after it gets pushed sideways? A scientist would call a balloon that quickly rights itself a stable balloon, but how do you make something stable? It has to do with where the weight is in the balloon.

Cut two 4-inch (10 cm) squares of thin cardboard (from a cereal box) and draw diagonal lines from each corner to find the center of each square. Push a thumbtack through the center of one square and put the other square over the top so the head of the thumbtack is sandwiched in the middle. Join the two squares together with tape along the edges. Carefully push the thumbtack into a cork message board so that the cards are held in place, yet free to spin around.

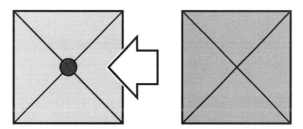

If you managed to get the pin exactly in the center, the spinning cards can come to rest with any side pointing up. And because the cards are balanced, they can spin for a long time and you can't tell where they will stop.

Now use a bit of poster putty or modeling clay to attach a penny to the center of the cards. The cards should still spin around easily, and if the penny is exactly in the middle, the cards will still come to rest in any position.

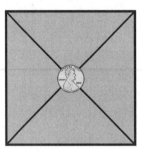

Move the penny so that its edge lies at the center of the cards. When you spin the card this time, it won't spin for nearly as long and will always come to rest with the penny underneath the pin. If you flick the card it will swing back so the penny is at the bottom again, maybe swinging back and forth a couple of times.

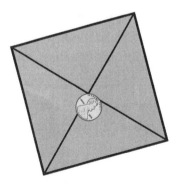

Next, move the penny so that it is right down in the corner of the cards. Now when you try and spin the card, it will probably only go around once and then quickly settle. So, the farther away the penny is from the pin, the quicker the card settles, and a heavier weight would also make the card settle more quickly.

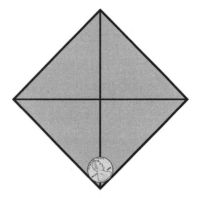

A balloon doesn't have a pin through the middle, but it does swing around a fixed point: the middle of the volume of hot air. Imagine a gas balloon in the shape of a perfect sphere. It can revolve around so that it is any way up because no part of the skin is heavier than any other. But if you tape a penny to the balloon, the skin will roll around until the penny hangs down underneath.

So, the spherical balloon revolves about the middle of the gas volume. A cylinder-shaped hot air balloon like the Khom Loi also revolves around the middle of the hot air volume, but, like all hot air balloons, the envelope is open at the bottom. This means that the envelope is not balanced: there is a circle of paper missing from the bottom of the envelope. This makes the envelope heavier at the top than at the bottom, so that if you fill the paper envelope of a Khom Loi with hot air, it tries to turn upside down.

All of the hot air balloons in this book suffer from this problem. The shape of the envelope puts a little bit more weight at the top of the balloon than at the bottom, so all these designs are unstable when filled with hot air. They need an extra weight at the bottom to make sure that the balloon stays upright. You add the weight by fixing a wire ring around the opening at the bottom of the balloon—the farthest point away from the center of the hot air—so that the weight can be as small as possible while still keeping the balloon upright.

Some balloons are more nearly balanced than others. The long, tapered shape of the Kongming Lantern envelope puts more hot air toward the top of the envelope so it is very nearly balanced; it needs only a thin wire ring to keep it upright.

How to Make the Montgolfiere

Adult supervision required

Materials

Newspaper or wallpaper to make a template

Thin clear tape, lightweight masking tape, or similar

12 sheets of tissue paper, 20 inches (50 cm) by 26 inches (66 cm) or larger

1 cup (240 mL) diluted white craft glue (1 part PVA glue to 5 parts water)

Undiluted white craft glue (PVA glue)

¼-inch (6 mm) hardwood dowel, 5 feet (1.5 m) long

Empty cereal boxes (or other source of thin cardboard)

Cotton ball (or balls), large enough to make a wad 3 inches (75 mm) long by 1½ inches (38 mm) wide

Aluminum foil

1 fluid ounce (30 mL) kerosene

Tools

Ruler

Pen

Scissors

Narrow sponge or brush (to apply glue)

8 or 10 straight (dressmaker's) pins

Heavy books or food cans to hold down the tissue paper

Hobby knife

8 clothespins

Before You Start

You will need a large, flat surface to build your balloon. You can use a table or the floor, but whatever you use you is going to get glue on it, so make sure the glue won't damage it. You can help to protect the table or floor by cutting trash bags into large plastic sheets to cover the work area.

If you do cover your table with plastic sheets, you can leave the balloon on the table to dry, as white craft glue will not stick to the plastic used to make trash bags. The balloon will dry more slowly if you leave it on the table rather than hang it up, but it is a lot easier.

As with any tissue paper balloon, it is a good idea to **have the bottom 12 inches (30 cm) of the balloon coated with a fire retardant**. You need to coat the tissue paper before you create the balloon—see chapter 11 (page 221) for instructions.

When you make a tissue paper balloon, most of your time is spent waiting for the glue to dry. If you have a blow-dryer, you can make a balloon much more quickly by using the blow-dryer to blow warm air at the glued seams. ***Don't use a fan heater or other room heater as they can set the tissue paper on fire.***

What to Do If Things Go Wrong

Holes in the tissue paper are easy to fix, and the Montgolfiere will still fly well. You can find repair instructions in chapter 11 (page 211).

In fact, check chapter 11 if you have accidentally glued parts of the panels that shouldn't be glued together, if you need a recipe for a different glue, if you cannot find the right materials, or if you have any other problems.

How to Make the Envelope

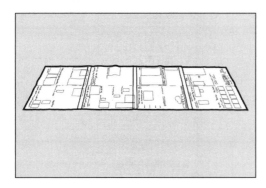

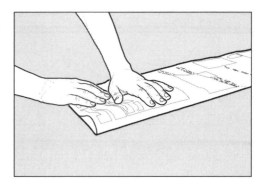

1. Tape together sheets of newspaper or cut a length of wallpaper large enough to make a template 50 inches (127 cm) long by 18 inches (46 cm) wide.

2. Fold the sheet in half along its length. Position the sheet so that the fold is toward you.

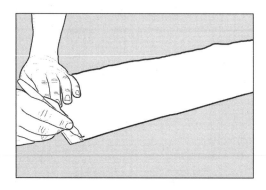

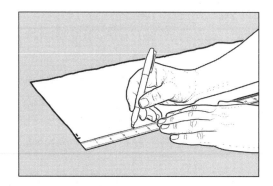

3. Put a ruler along the left-hand edge and make a mark ¾ inch (19 mm) up from the fold. This is point 1 from the table below.

4. Measure 4⅛ inches (105 mm) along the fold from the left-hand end and make a mark on the fold.

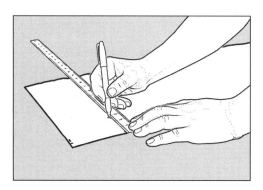

5. Measure 2⅞ inches (73 mm) across the sheet from the mark you made in step 4 and draw a small cross. This cross is point 2 from the table on the right.

Template Measurements

Point	Distance Along Fold	Distance Across from Fold
1	0	¾ inches (19 mm)
2	4⅛ inches (105 mm)	2⅞ inches (73 mm)
3	8¼ inches (210 mm)	4⅞ inches (124 mm)
4	12⅜ inches (314 mm)	6⅝ inches (168 mm)
5	16½ inches (419 mm)	7⅞ inches (200 mm)
6	20⅝ inches (524 mm)	8¾ inches (222 mm)
7	24¾ inches (629 mm)	9 inches (229 mm)
8	29 inches (737 mm)	8¾ inches (222 mm)
9	49¼ inches (1,251 mm)	5⅞ inches (149 mm)

Repeat steps 4 and 5 for each of the rows in the table, measuring along the fold by the distance in the middle column and then across the sheet by the distance in the right-hand column.

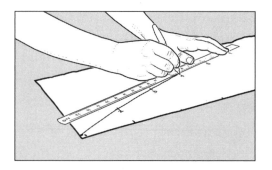

6. Draw a line from point 1 to point 2 and then continue the line to join all of the numbered points together. When you get to point 9, draw a line straight down to the fold.

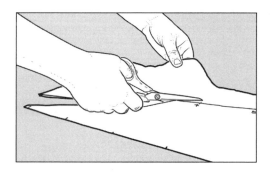

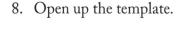

7. Cut along the line that you drew in step 6.

8. Open up the template.

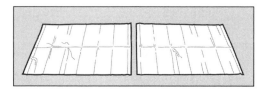

9. Put two sheets of tissue paper on a large table or on the floor. Arrange them so they meet along their narrow edges.

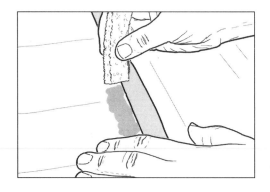

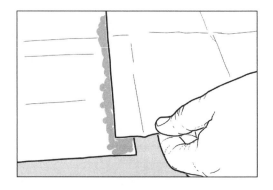

10. Wet a narrow sponge (or brush) with diluted glue and squeeze it out. Apply the glue to the edge of the left-hand sheet of tissue paper.

11. Lift the right-hand sheet of tissue paper across, line it up over the glued edge, and press down.

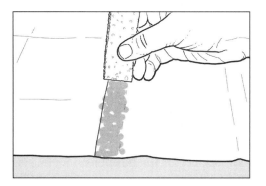

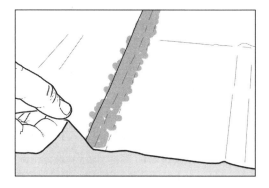

12. Apply more diluted glue to the seam so that it soaks through both sheets. This will glue together any area that may not have stuck when you pressed the sheets together.

13. Gently lift the left-hand sheet of tissue paper so that both sheets peel away from the table or floor. Put the pair of tissue paper sheets over the back of a chair or over a door so that they can dry. Repeat steps 9 to 13 until you have six long tissue paper sheets.

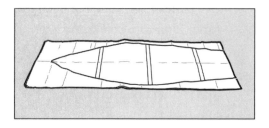

14. When the long sheets are dry, put all six of them in a stack with the template on top. If the balloon panels are to be alternating colors, then lay the long tissue paper sheets in the stack in alternating colors. Arrange the sheets so the right-hand edges line up.

15. Hold the template and long tissue paper sheets together with straight pins.

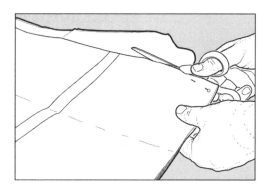

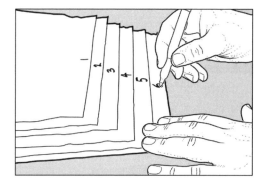

16. Cut around the template with a sharp pair of scissors to make six tissue paper panels. Keep the tissue paper as close to the table or floor as possible while you cut so the panels will all be the same size.

17. Number the bottom of the panels from 1 to 6. The flat end will be the bottom of the panel.

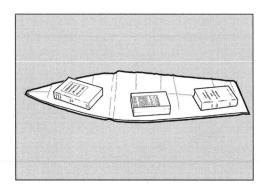

18. Lay panel 1 on the table or floor with panel 2 on top. Position the pointed end on the left and slide panel 2 away from you to expose a strip of panel 1 that's ½ inch (13 mm) wide. Make sure that the exposed strip of panel 1 is even along its length, and put some heavy books or food cans on top to keep the panels from moving.

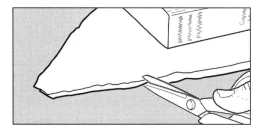

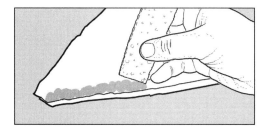

19. Use a pair of scissors to carefully cut the exposed edge of panel 1 into flaps, each approximately 4 inches (10 cm) long.

20. With the sponge, dab diluted glue along the edge of panel 2 to make a wet strip ½ inch (13 mm) wide next to the first panel 1 flap.

21. Fold up the panel 1 flap and pat it down onto the glued strip of panel 2.

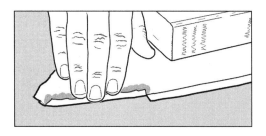

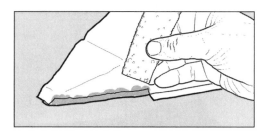 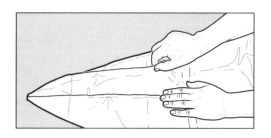

22. Use the sponge to re-wet the flap. This will glue down any dry patches so there are no leaky gaps. Repeat steps 20 to 22 until the entire seam has been glued. Peel the envelope off the table or floor and put it somewhere to dry. Clean any glue from the work area.

23. When the seam is dry, put the envelope back on the table or floor with panel 2 on the bottom. Make sure that the pointed end (the top of the envelope) is still on your left-hand side. Fold back the top panel (panel 1) so that the free edges line up with the seam at the back of the envelope. Make a neat crease down the middle. This puts panel 1 safely out of the way and leaves panel 2 exposed so it is easy to join to panel 3.

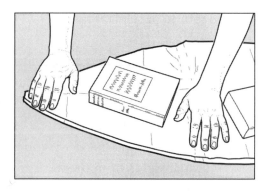

24. Lay panel 3 on top of the envelope. Again, slide panel 3 away from you to expose a strip of panel 2 that's ½ inch (13 mm) wide. Arrange panel 3 so that the exposed strip is even along its length and put heavy books or food cans on top.

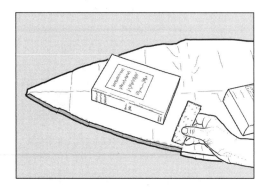

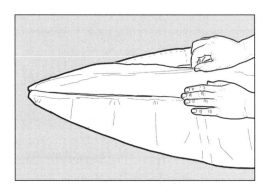

25. Cut, paste, fold, and glue as you did in steps 19 to 22 to form a seam. Peel the envelope off the table or floor and put it aside to dry. Clean any glue from the work area before it dries.

26. When the seam is dry, put the envelope back on the table or floor with panel 3 on the bottom. Make sure that the pointed end (the top of the envelope) is still on your left-hand side. Fold back panels 1 and 2 so that the free edges line up with the seam at the back of the envelope. Make a neat crease down the middle. This puts panels 1 and 2 safely out of the way and leaves panel 3 exposed so it is easy to join to panel 4.

27. Lay panel 4 carefully on top of the envelope. Cut, glue, fold, and glue again as you did in steps 19 to 22 to form a seam. Peel the envelope off the table or floor and put it aside to dry. Clean any glue from the work area before it dries.

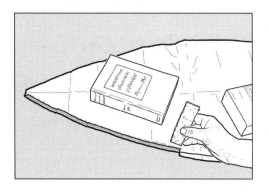

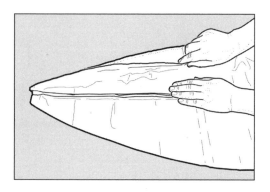 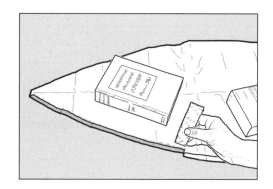

28. When the envelope is dry, put it back on the table or floor with panel 4 on the bottom and the pointed top end on the left. Fold back panels 1, 2, and 3 so that the edges all line up at the back of the envelope. Press down to form a neat crease.

29. Position panel 5 carefully on top of the envelope. Cut, glue, fold, and glue again as you did in steps 19 to 22 to form a seam. Peel the envelope off the table or floor and put it aside to dry. Clean any glue from the work area before it dries.

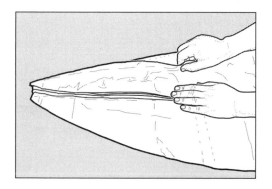

30. When the assembly is dry, put it back on the table or floor with panel 5 on the bottom and the pointed top end on the left. Fold back panels 1, 2, 3, and 4 so that the edges all line up at the back of the envelope. Press down to form a neat crease.

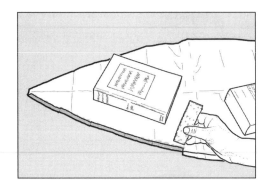

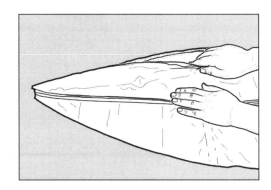

31. Position panel 6 carefully on top of the envelope. Cut, glue, fold, and glue again as you did in steps 19 to 22 to form a seam. Peel the envelope off the table or floor and put it aside to dry. Clean any glue from the work area before it dries.

32. When the envelope is dry, put it back on the table or floor with panel 6 on the bottom and the pointed top end on the left. Fold back panels 1, 2, 3, 4, and 5 so that the edges all line up at the back of the envelope. Press down to form a neat crease.

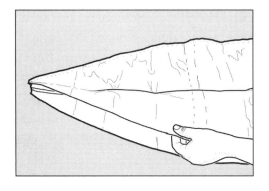

33. Take panel 1 from the top of the stack at the back of the envelope and fold it forward over panel 6.

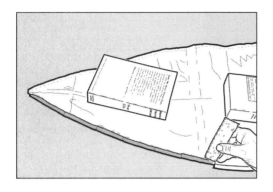

34. Position panel 1 carefully on top of the envelope. You may have to hold panel 1 down with heavy books or food cans as it can be pulled out of place by the other panels. Cut, glue, fold, and glue again as you did in steps 19 to 22 to form a seam. Peel the envelope off the table or floor and put it aside to dry. Clean any glue from the work area before it dries.

How to Make the Wire-Free Burner

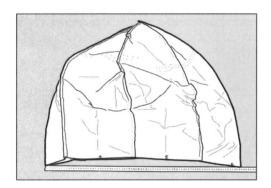

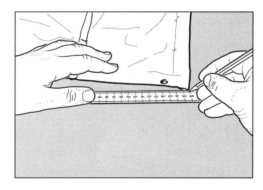

35. Flatten out the envelope and place a ruler along the base. Make sure that the seams run down the middle of the envelope and not at the sides or it will be hard to measure the opening accurately.

36. Measure across the opening.

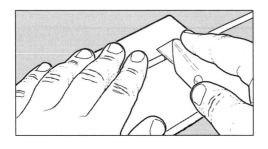

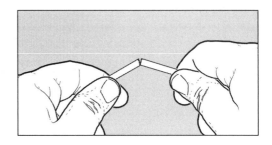

37. Make a mark at half this distance along a length of dowel, then use a sharp knife to score all the way around at this mark.

38. Snap the dowel at the scored line. Repeat so you have two dowels.

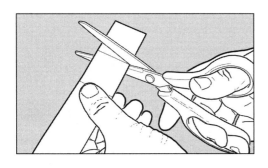

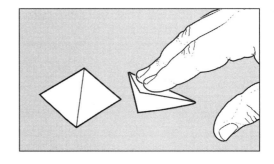

39. Cut two 2-inch (5 cm) squares from an empty cereal box or other piece of thin cardboard.

40. Fold these squares in half across a diagonal line.

41. Attach one square onto the center of each dowel using undiluted glue.

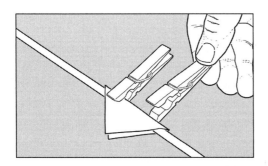

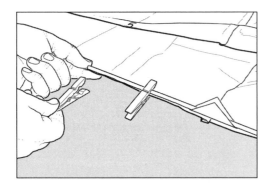

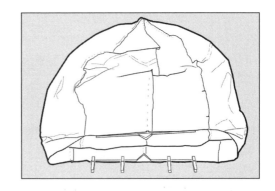

42. Glue one dowel into the inside edge of the opening. Line up the card triangle with one of the seams. This will make it easier to get the second dowel glued into the opening exactly opposite the first one. Hold the rod in place using clothespins.

43. Glue the second dowel into the inside edge of the opening. Line up the cardboard triangle with the seam in the envelope so the dowels are exactly opposite one another.

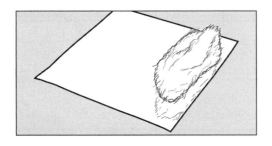

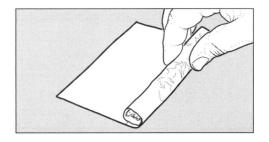

44. Lay a piece of cotton ball about 3 inches (75 mm) long by 1½ inches (38 mm) wide onto a 6-inch (15 cm) square of aluminum foil. If you cannot find a large enough piece of cotton ball, pack individual cotton balls together.

45. Roll the aluminum foil into a tube.

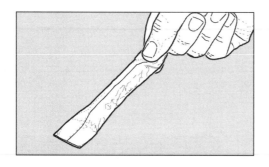

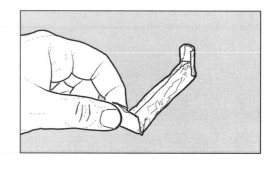

46. Position the seam at the top and flatten both ends into a flap.

47. Bend the flaps up and fold the sides of the flaps along either side of the tube as shown.

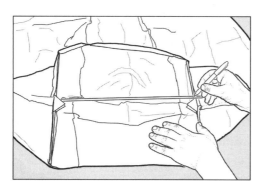

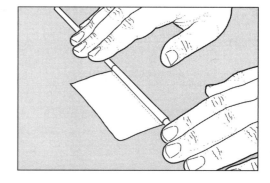

48. Lay a third dowel across the opening at the bottom of the envelope. Mark and cut the dowel so it will just fit in between the two rods already fixed into the opening.

49. Wrap a 4-inch (10 cm) square piece of aluminum foil around the center of the third dowel. If it springs away from the rod after you let go, tighten it again and hold the edge down with a small piece of tape.

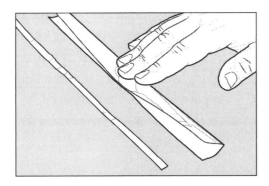

50. Cut a 2-inch-by-12-inch (5 cm by 30 cm) piece of aluminum foil and fold it along its length. Fold the foil another two times to make an aluminum strip just under ¼ inch (6 mm) wide.

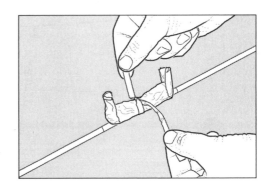

51. Place the foil-covered cotton-ball burner on top of the foil-covered part of the third dowel. Make sure that the seam in the burner is on top and tie it securely onto the rod using the foil strip. Cut the ends of the strip close to the knot.

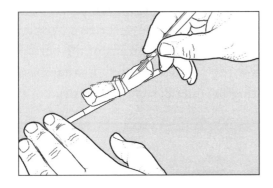

52. Use a sharp knife to cut away two windows in the top half of the foil roll. Leave the foil under the strip.

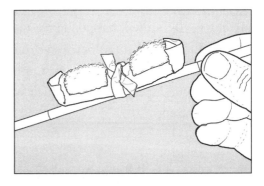

53. The completed burner is attached to the third dowel.

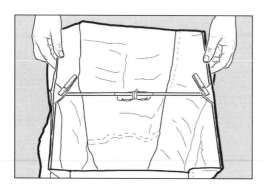

54. Spread undiluted glue onto the insides of the cardboard triangles and slip the ends of the third dowel between the triangles. Make sure that the burner is pointing into the balloon. Use clothespins to hold the dowel in place.

What to Do Next

Check the envelope for any leaks by inflating it over an electric toaster or blow-dryer. Look for gaps in the seams or holes in the tissue paper and repair them (see instructions in chapter 11, page 211). Take care not to scorch the cotton ball in the burner or the exposed wood in the base frame. Once you have fixed any leaks, the balloon is complete and ready to fly. See chapter 2 for instructions on flying a balloon with a burner.

Applying a fire retardant to the tissue paper will almost completely eliminate burn-ups on launching. If the wind catches the burner flame and pushes it onto the side of the envelope, all that will happen is the flame will scorch a hole through the tissue paper.

Because the Montgolfiere envelope has a lot of lift, you can use any of the burners in this book. To use a burner supported by a wire you will need to fit a rattan base ring (chapter 7, page 138) or a thick wire base ring (chapter 8, page 164) instead of the wooden frame.

A Larger Montgolfiere

If you want to make a larger and more elegantly shaped Montgolfiere envelope, start by taping together a strip of newspaper large enough to make a 75-inch-by-20-inch (190 cm by 50 cm) template. Use the following table to make the template:

Template Measurements

Point	Distance Along Fold	Distance Across from Fold
1	0	¾ inches (19 mm)
2	4⅛ inches (105 mm)	2⅞ inches (73 mm)
3	8¼ inches (210 mm)	4⅞ inches (124 mm)
4	12⅜ inches (314 mm)	6⅝ inches (168 mm)
5	16½ inches (419 mm)	7⅞ inches (200 mm)
6	20⅝ inches (524 mm)	8¾ inches (222 mm)
7	24¾ inches (629 mm)	9 inches (229 mm)
8	29 inches (737 mm)	8⅞ inches (225 mm)
9	49¼ inches (1,251 mm)	5⅞ inches (149 mm)

You then need to join together three sheets of tissue paper by gluing them together along their narrow edges, like this:

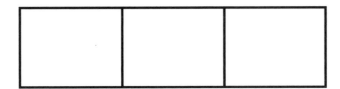

Repeat this until you have six long sheets of tissue paper and then follow the instructions in this chapter starting with step 14.

7
The Khom Loi

The Khom Loi in this book is a cylindrical balloon about 53 inches (1.3 m) tall and about 25 inches (64 cm) in diameter. It is made from four panels of tissue paper glued together with a circular tissue paper top. The balloon has a circular ring glued into the opening at the bottom made from rattan cane or split bamboo.

The Khom Loi has a special burner made from string wound into a thick ring and soaked in wax. The burner is supported on thin wires stretched across the rattan ring at the bottom of the Khom Loi.

The envelope of the Khom Loi is easy to put together, but you will need to use a calculator to determine how big to make the circular tissue paper top. *You will need to*

take care not to get wax on yourself when melting wax for the burner, especially when soaking the string burner itself in the hot wax. Heatproof gloves and safety glasses are essential.

The large cylindrical shape means that the Khom Loi contains a lot of air, so it has a lot of lift. This means that the balloon can lift a heavier burner, giving a longer flight and a rapid climb. However, because the Khom Loi is not tapered and has a large opening in the bottom, it does need a heavier base ring than either the Kongming Lantern or the Montgolfiere designs.

Traditional Khom Loi Designs

Khom Loi (floating lantern) and Khom Fai (fire lantern) are general names given to any paper hot air balloon in Thailand. The Thai people use a number of different designs during their festivals, but the cylindrical design shown on the previous page is one of the most common. Another common design has four straight-sided panels formed with a pointed end so that the panels can be glued together in much the same way as the Kongming Lantern and the balloon needs no separate top.

Thai Khom Loi are often made from rice paper, sometimes oiled to make it more airtight. The rice paper used to make the balloons is not the edible rice paper made from rice flour and tapioca, but a thin and very strong paper made from the bark of the mulberry tree. It is called rice paper because the thicker grades are used to make the sacks for storing rice. Tissue paper is a good alternative if rice paper is unavailable, although it is not as strong.

Thai balloons use a lot of different burner designs. Some burners have fabric patches soaked in wax; some have bundles of fibers like the burner in this chapter. One common type of burner is made by soaking wax into a roll of toilet tissue and then cutting off 1-inch (25 mm) rings like slices of bread. You suspend one of the rings in the middle of the base ring using thin wires. Whatever wax burner is used, the secret to getting it to light is to have a thin piece of stuff sticking out to act as a wick or touch-paper. With the toilet roll burner you unpeel a bit of the first few sheets; with the string burner you have a few inches of string sticking out from the ring.

Measuring Air Density

Because you know how a gas expands and shrinks with temperature, you can use the lift from a hot air balloon to make an estimate of air density. To make the calculation you need to know the volume of the balloon, the temperature inside the balloon, the room temperature, the weight of the balloon, and the strength of the lift. It is important that the temperature inside the balloon and the lift are calculated at the same time, as they can go up and down quite quickly.

Measuring the lift is actually very easy. The trick is to put a 100-gram weight onto a set of electronic weighing scales and attach the balloon to the weight using thin sewing thread. When the balloon is lifting upward, the weight displayed by the electronic scales will appear to go down. You calculate the lift by figuring out how much weight has been "lost." It is even easier if you use the zeroing or "tare" function. After you have tied the thread to the 100-gram weight and put it on the scales, you press the "zero" button and the display then reads zero. Now when the balloon pulls upward, the scales will give a direct reading of the lift (with a minus sign in front of the number).

The Khom Loi from this chapter is an ideal choice to use in this experiment, as it has a simple cylindrical shape. You only need to measure the diameter and the height to be able to calculate the volume inside the balloon.

You should heat the air inside with an electric heater rather than a wax or kerosene burner. The burner gets lighter as the fuel is used, so you cannot calculate the overall lift.

To measure the temperature inside the balloon, you are going to need a thermometer with a higher range than a normal room thermometer; the temperature inside the balloon can reach as high as 150°C (300°F). You can use some cheap oven thermometers (though make sure the thermometer reads down to about 50°C, or 120°F), a sugar thermometer for making jam and jelly (this is ideal), or a soil thermometer.

But the main difficulty is reading the scale on your thermometer when it is in position—right up at the top of your balloon. The simplest way is to cut out a small rectangle of paper from the side of the balloon and tape a clear polyethylene window into place. You can then read the thermometer through the side of the balloon. If you can get hold of a thermocouple temperature probe, or an oven thermometer with a separate display, then you can hold the probe inside the balloon and run the wire down through the opening at the bottom of the envelope.

Whatever type of thermometer you use, you will need to mount it on a stick so you can hold it up at the top of the balloon for long enough to make an accurate measurement without blocking the hot air going into the bottom of the envelope.

Materials

Khom Loi envelope with base ring (but no burner fitted)

Clear plastic bag

Thin clear tape, lightweight masking tape, or similar

Oven thermometer or similar

Room thermometer

Length of dowel or other stick to hold oven thermometer

Sewing thread

100-gram weight

Tools

Scissors

Ruler

Electronic scales

Pen

Paper or notepad

Electric toaster or similar electric heater

Making the Measurements

1. Cut a 4-inch (10 cm) square hole in the side of the Khom Loi envelope next to the top. Cut a 5-inch (127 mm) square from the clear plastic bag. Carefully tape the clear plastic square over the hole to form a window into the Khom Loi, making sure the pieces of tape cross over each other to prevent any leaks.

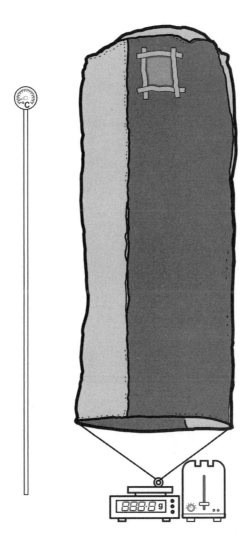

2. Weigh the Khom Loi in grams.
3. Tape the oven thermometer onto the end of the dowel so that you can read the dial through the window in the Khom Loi.

4. Attach a piece of sewing thread across the opening of the Khom Loi. The thread must be about twice as long as the diameter of the Khom Loi so it hangs down in a loop. Tie or tape the 100-gram weight to the center of the thread and put the weight onto the pan of your scales.
5. Zero the scales or write down the weight.
6. Put the electric toaster next to the scales, support the Khom Loi over the toaster, and turn on the toaster.
7. When the balloon is pulling upward strongly, put the oven thermometer up into the balloon so that the dial can be seen through the window in the side of the Khom Loi.
8. Wait until the thermometer settles to the new temperature.
9. Quickly write down the weight reported by the scales, the temperature inside the balloon, and the room temperature.

How to Calculate the Result

To calculate the density of air from the experimental measurements, you need to use a mathematical formula that describes how the air behaves when heated. The formula is called the Ideal Gas Law, and it is usually written as:

$$pV = NkT$$

Where p is the gas pressure, V is the volume, N is the number of gas molecules, k is a fixed number called the Boltzmann Constant, and T is the temperature in Kelvin. It is not very easy to use this formula to calculate air density from your experimental data, and you don't need to worry about the pressure effects as all of the experiment is done at atmospheric pressure. The formula is a lot easier to use if you simplify and rearrange it:

$$\text{Density} = \frac{\text{Gross Lift}}{\text{Volume} \times \left(1 - \dfrac{T_{room}}{T_{balloon}}\right)}$$

Where:

- Gross Lift is calculated by adding the measured lift from the electronic balance to the weight of the balloon. Gross lift must be in kilograms.
- Volume is the Khom Loi envelope volume in m^3.
- T_{room} is the temperature of the room measured in degrees Kelvin. To convert a temperature measured in Celsius to Kelvin, just add 273.
- $T_{balloon}$ is the temperature inside the balloon measured in degrees Kelvin.

It's time to look at an example. Here are some of my measurements to show you how to use the formula:

Measurements

Room Temperature: 20°C

Balloon Temperature: 90°C

Khom Loi Size: Diameter, 0.611 m; Height, 1.28 m

Khom Loi Weight: 0.048 kg

Measured Lift: 0.040 kg

Calculations

The Khom Loi volume can be calculated using the formula for the volume of a cylinder:

$$\text{Volume} = \pi\, r^2\, h = 3.14 \times 0.3055^2 \times 1.28 = 0.375 \text{ m}^3$$

Convert the room temperature to Kelvin by adding 273:

$$T_{room} = 20 + 273 = 293° \text{ K}$$

Convert the balloon temperature to Kelvin by adding 273:

$$T_{balloon} = 90 + 273 = 363° \text{ K}$$

The Gross Lift can be calculated by adding the envelope weight to the measured lift:

$$\text{Gross Lift} = 0.048 + 0.040 = 0.088 \text{ kg}$$

The air density is then calculated:

$$\text{Density} = \frac{\text{Gross Lift}}{\text{Volume} \times \left(1 - \dfrac{T_{room}}{T_{balloon}}\right)}$$

$$Density = 1.2 kg/m^3$$

How to Make the Khom Loi

Adult supervision required

Materials

10 sheets of tissue paper, 20 inches by 26 inches (50 cm by 66 cm) or larger

1 cup (240 mL) diluted white craft glue (1 part PVA glue to 5 parts water)

5 feet (1.5 m) fresh rattan center cane or split bamboo, ¼ inch (6 mm) diameter

5 feet (1.5 m) thin soft iron wire

⅓ ounce (10 g) soft jute string or soft cotton string

2 ounces (60 g) paraffin wax or beeswax

Tools

Narrow sponge or brush to apply glue

Pen

Ruler

Heavy books or food cans to keep the tissue paper from moving

Scissors

Clean sponge and dry cloth

Calculator to determine radius

Strip of cardboard, 40 inches (102 cm) long (to make a radius measure)

8 small pieces of cardboard, ¾ inches by 2 inches (2 cm by 5 cm), to hold ring in place

8 paper clips, to hold ring in place

Hobby knife

8 clothespins

Small jar, about 2½ inches (64 mm) in diameter, to wind string around for the burner

Large jar, about 4 inches (10 cm) in diameter, to melt wax

Heatproof gloves

Safety glasses

Pencil

Newspaper

Pliers (with wire cutters)

Before You Start

You will need a large, flat surface to build your balloon. You can use a table or the floor, but whatever you use is going to get glue on it, so make sure the glue won't damage it. You can help to protect the table or floor by cutting trash bags into large plastic sheets to cover the work area.

If you do cover your table with plastic sheets, you can leave the balloon on the table to dry, as white craft glue will not stick to the plastic used to make trash bags. The balloon will dry more slowly if you leave it on the table rather than hang it up, but it is a lot easier.

As with any tissue paper balloon, it is a good idea to **have the bottom 12 inches (30 cm) of the balloon coated with a fire retardant**. You need to coat the tissue paper before you create the balloon—see chapter 11 (page 221) for instructions.

When you make a tissue paper balloon, most of your time is spent waiting for the glue to dry. If you have a blow-dryer, you can make a balloon much more quickly by using the blow-dryer to blow warm air at the glued seams. **Don't use a fan heater or other room heater as they can set the tissue paper on fire.**

What to Do If Things Go Wrong

Holes in the tissue paper are easy to fix, and the Khom Loi will still fly well. You can find repair instructions in chapter 11 (page 211).

In fact, check chapter 11 if you have glued parts of the panels that shouldn't be glued together, if you need a recipe for a different glue, if you cannot find the right materials, or if you have any other problems.

How to Make a Tissue Paper Cylinder

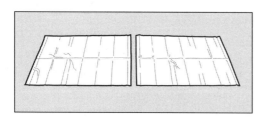

1. Put two sheets of tissue paper on a large table or on the floor. Arrange them so that they meet along their narrow edges.

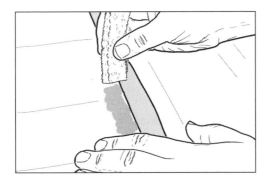

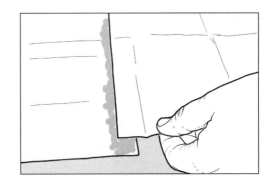

2. Wet a narrow sponge (or brush) with diluted glue and squeeze it out so that it is nearly dry. Apply glue to the edge of the left-hand sheet of tissue paper.

3. Lift the right-hand sheet of tissue paper across, line it up over the glued edge, and press down.

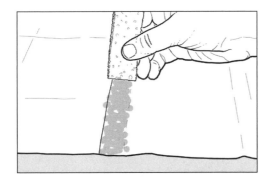

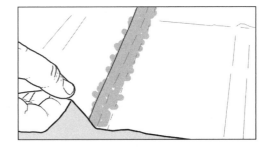

4. Apply more glue to the seam so that it soaks through both sheets. This will glue together any dry patches.

5. Gently lift the left-hand sheet of tissue paper so that both sheets peel away from the table or floor. Put the pair of tissue paper sheets over the back of a chair or over a door so that they can dry. Repeat these steps until you have four panels made from pairs of tissue paper sheets.

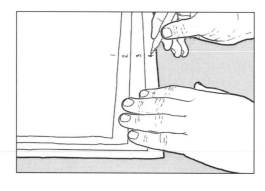

6. Number panels on their bottom edges.

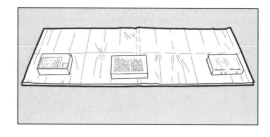

7. Lay panel 1 on the table or floor with panel 2 on top. Slide panel 2 away from you so that there is a ½-inch (13 mm) strip of panel 1 showing. Put books or food cans on top to keep the panels in place.

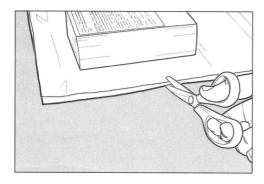

8. Make a series of cuts spaced 4 inches (10 cm) apart across the projecting strip of the lower panel. Make sure that you only cut across the projecting strip and not into the upper panel.

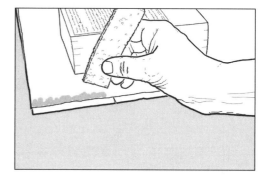

9. Wet the narrow sponge with diluted glue and squeeze it out so that it is nearly dry. Dab the sponge along the edge of the top panel to make a strip about ½ inch (13 mm) wide, wet with glue.

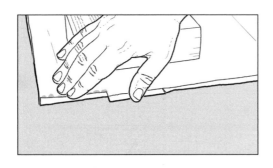

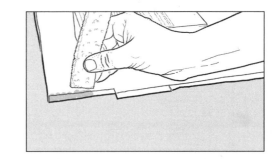

10. Fold up the flap and pat down onto the glued strip.

11. Dab the sponge over the flap to stick down any dry patches. Continue with the rest of the flaps until you finish the seam. Peel the envelope off the table or floor and hang it over the back of a chair to dry. Wipe the glue from the work area with a clean sponge and dry with a cloth.

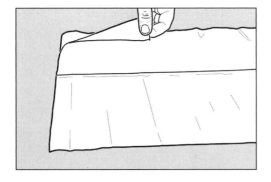

12. When the seam is dry, put the envelope back on the table or floor with panel 2 on the bottom. Make sure that numbered ends are on your right-hand side. Fold back the top panel (panel 1) so that the free edges line up with the seam at the back of the envelope. Make a neat crease down the middle. This puts panel 1 safely out of the way and leaves panel 2 exposed so it is easy to join to panel 3.

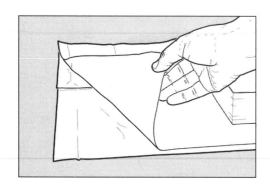

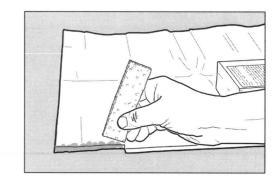

13. Lay panel 3 on top of the envelope and slide it away from you to expose a strip of panel 2 at the front that's ½ inch (13 mm) wide. Make sure that the strip is even along its length and put books or food cans on top to keep the panels in place.

14. Make a seam as you did in steps 8 to 11. Peel the envelope off the table or floor, hang it up to dry, and clean the work area.

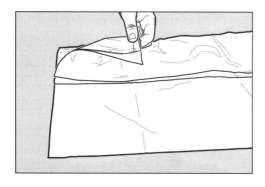

15. When the seam is dry, put the envelope back on the table or floor with panel 3 on the bottom. Make sure that numbered ends are on your right-hand side. Fold back panels 1 and 2 so that the free edges line up with the seams at the back of the envelope. Make a neat crease down the middle.

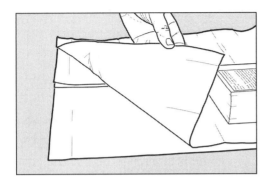

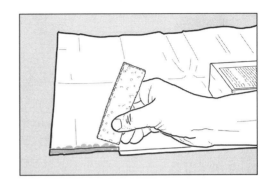

16. Lay panel 4 on top of the assembly and slide the panel away from you to expose a ½-inch (13 mm) strip of panel 3 at the front. Make sure that the strip is even along its length and put books or food cans on top to keep the panels in place.

17. Make a seam as you did in steps 8 to 11. Peel the envelope off the table or floor, hang it up to dry, and clean the work area.

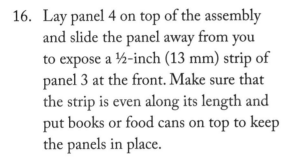

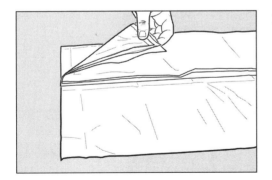

18. When the seam is dry, put the envelope back on the table or floor with panel 4 on the bottom. Make sure that numbered ends are on your right-hand side. Fold back panels 1, 2, and 3 so that the free edges line up with the seams at the back of the envelope. Make a neat crease down the middle.

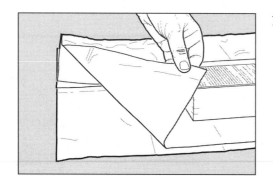

19. Take the edge of the top panel on the stack (panel 1) and fold it forward again over the bottom panel (panel 4). Line up the top panel to expose a ½-inch (13 mm) strip of the bottom panel. This will be more difficult than before as the back edge of the top panel is already joined to the envelope. Use heavy books or food cans to hold the top panel in place.

20. Make a seam as you did in steps 8 to 11. Peel the envelope off the table or floor, hang it up to dry, and clean the work area.

How to Fit a Circular Top

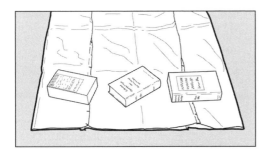

21. When the envelope is dry, flatten it out onto the table or floor with the seams running down the middle so no seams are at the sides.

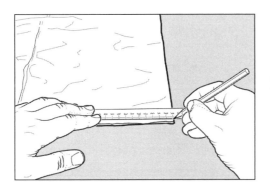

22. Measure across the inside of the opening at the top end (the end without any numbers).

23. Multiply the measurement of the opening by 3.14 (use a calculator) and then add on another ¾ inch (2 cm) to get the radius of the paper circle that will form the top of the Khom Loi. The extra ¾ inch is to allow for the seam that joins the circle to the body.

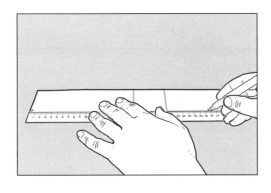

24. Take a long strip of cardboard and mark one corner. Make a second mark so that the distance between the two marks is the same as the radius calculated in step 23. You will use this piece of cardboard to draw the paper circle before you cut it out.

25. Glue two sheets of tissue paper together so that they are joined along their long edges.

26. When the sheet is dry, measure along the seam to find the center of the sheet. Mark it with a small *X*.

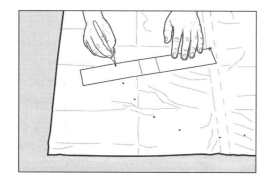

27. Take the strip of cardboard that you prepared in step 24 and put the marked corner on the *X* in the center of the tissue paper. Make a mark on the tissue paper next to the second mark on the cardboard strip. Swing the cardboard strip around so that the marked corner still lies on the *X* in the center of the tissue paper. Make another mark on the tissue paper 3 or 4 inches (75 or 100 mm) from the first one. Continue until you have a circle of marks.

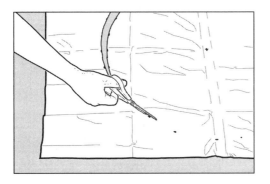 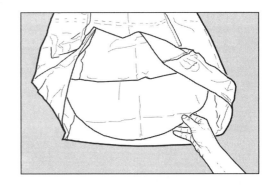

28. Cut from mark to mark to make a circle of tissue paper.

29. Put the envelope back on the table or floor and flatten it out. Push the paper circle inside the top of the envelope and position the top edge of the circle ¾ inch (2 cm) inside the edge of the envelope.

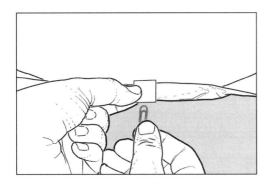

30. Fold ¾ inch (2 cm) of the envelope over the tissue paper circle and hold it in place with a fixing made from a folded-over piece of cardboard and a paper clip.

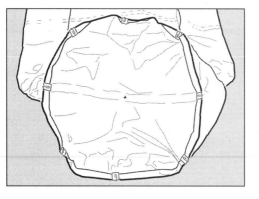

31. Repeat until there are a total of eight fixings evenly spaced around the top of the body. If you glue all of gaps between the fixings, the tissue paper would get so weak that the circle would rip off when you tried to lift the envelope off the table or floor. Instead you are going to glue alternate gaps between fixings.

Put the envelope onto the table or floor with one of the gaps at the front. Make sure that the edge of the envelope is pulled well forward so that there are no folds of tissue paper trapped underneath.

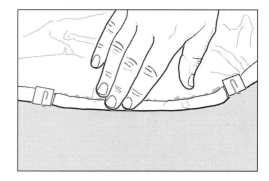

32. Tear the edge of the envelope in between two of the fixings so the tissue paper forms a flap. Glue a ½-inch (13 mm) strip along the edge of the circle next to the flap.

33. Fold the flap back up over the edge of the circle and pat the flap down onto the glued strip.

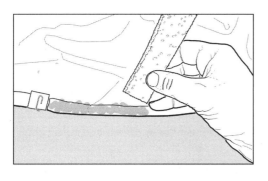

34. Rewet the flap with glue to fix any dry parts of the seam. Lift the envelope off the table or floor and clean any glue that seeped onto the work area.

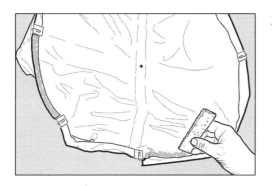

35. Reposition the envelope so the ring lies a quarter-turn around with a new gap at the front. This leaves an unglued gap between the gap you have already glued and the one you are about to glue. Tear the paper on either side of the gap and fold down the flap. Glue the flap into place in the same way that you did in steps 32 to 34. Repeat this until four gaps have been glued. Put the envelope to one side and leave it to dry.

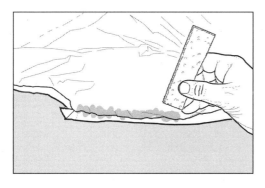

36. When the envelope is dry, remove all of the fixings and put it back on the table or floor. Glue the remaining flaps into place in the same way that you did in steps 32 to 34.

How to Fit a Rattan Base Ring

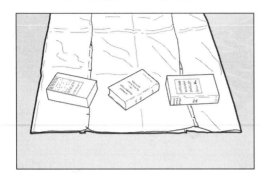

37. When the envelope is dry, flatten it out onto the table or floor with the seams running down the middle, so that no seams are at the sides.

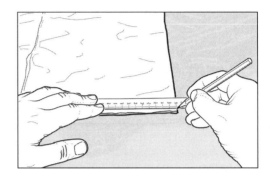

38. Measure across the inside of the opening at the bottom end (the end with the numbers).

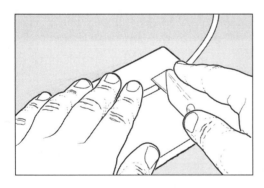

39. Make a mark twice this distance along a piece of rattan cane. Score all around the cane at the mark using a sharp knife.

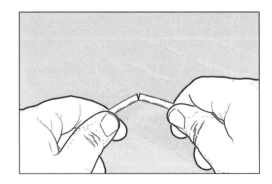

40. Snap the cane at the scored mark.

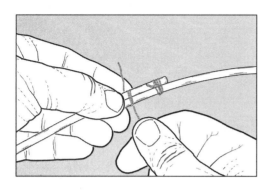

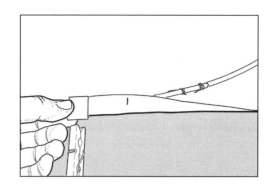

41. Bend the cane around in a circle and overlap the ends by 2 inches (5 cm). Wind soft wire around the seam at two places and twist together. Bend the twists to lie against the cane as shown. Then lay the envelope on the table or floor and put the rattan base ring inside the opening at the base.

42. Fold ¾ inch (2 cm) of the lower edge over the rattan base ring, fold a small piece of cardboard over the tissue paper, and hold it in place with a clothespin.

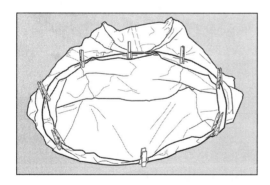

43. Repeat until you have eight pegs evenly spaced around the base ring. Lay the balloon flat on the table or floor with the ring on top. Draw the lower edge toward you to ensure that none of the envelope is trapped underneath.

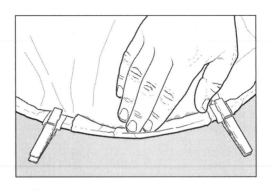

44. Tear the lower edge of the balloon between two of the pegs to form a flap. Fold the flap down onto the table or floor and glue the tissue paper above the ring as shown. Make sure that the glue doesn't stick the tissue paper to the cardboard fixing.

45. Fold the flap back up and pat onto the wet tissue paper.

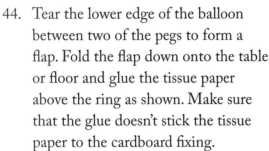

46. Rewet the flap to glue together any dry patches. Keep the glue away from the cardboard fixings. Lift the balloon off the table or floor and clean the glue from the work area.

You are going to glue half of the gaps just as you did when gluing the paper circle into the top of the envelope. Lay the balloon back down on the table or floor with the next gap toward you. Tear down a flap and glue it as before. Repeat these steps until you have glued half of the gaps. Put the balloon to one side and prop the base ring up until the glued flaps are dry. Once the flaps are all dry, remove all of the clothespins and cardboard.

47. Glue the remaining flaps in the same way and put the completed balloon to one side to dry.

How to Make a Waxed String Burner

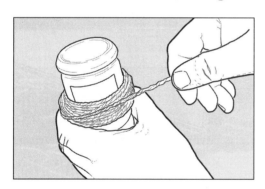

48. Wind about ⅓ ounce (10 g) of soft jute string around a small jam jar to form a thick ring. Slip the ring off the jam jar.

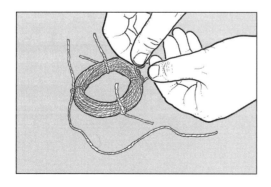

49. Tie string around the side of the ring at three or four places so that the ring will hold together. Leave one of the strings long so that the ring can be hung from it. Cut the other strings to about 2 inches (5 cm) long. After being coated with wax, these strings will form wicks to make the burner easy to light.

50. Partially fill a jam jar with wax blocks (at least 2 ounces, or 60 g). ***Ask an adult*** to help you melt the wax. See chapter 11 for instructions on how to melt wax (page 219).

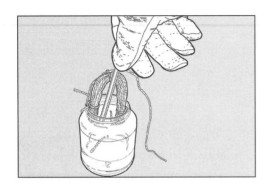 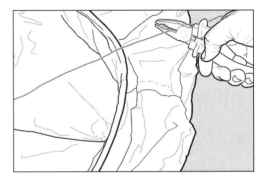

51. Put on heatproof gloves and safety glasses and take the jam jar out of the oven. Hold the jam jar down onto a heatproof surface with one gloved hand and push the string burner down into the wax with a pencil. You will have to squash the burner to get it into the jar, and you may have to take it out and turn it around to get all of the string soaked in wax. Use the long string to pull the burner out of the jam jar, and lay the burner on a clean piece of newspaper to cool and harden.

52. Stretch a thin iron wire across the base ring and cut it 6 inches (15 cm) beyond the edge of the base ring. Repeat this so that you have two pieces of wire.

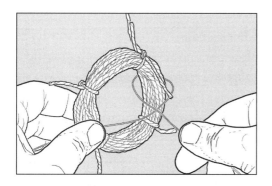

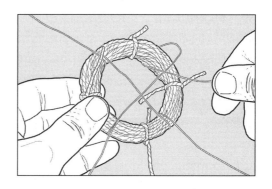

53. Take one of the wires and place the burner in the middle. Pass one end of the wire around the side of the ring and through the center. Pull the wire tight and repeat with the other end of the wire.

54. Lay the other wire across the burner at right angles to the first wire and loop the ends around the side of the burner ring in the same way.

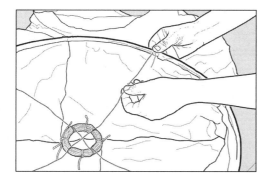

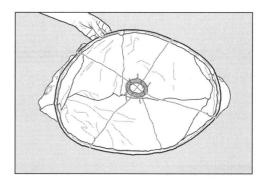

55. Put the burner in the center of the base ring. Take one of the wires from the burner and push the free end through the tissue paper just above the base ring. Bend the wire around the base ring and then twist the free end back around the burner wire to secure it.

56. Repeat with the wire on the opposite side of the burner, being careful to keep the burner in the center of the base ring. Repeat with the other two wires. Cut off any excess from the free ends of the burner wires.

What Next?

Check the envelope for any leaks by inflating it over an electric toaster or blow-dryer. Look for gaps in the seams or holes in the tissue paper and repair them (see instructions in chapter 11, page 211). ***Take care that the hot air from the toaster does not melt the wax or it will drip off and may set the toaster on fire.*** Once you have fixed any leaks, the balloon is complete and ready to fly. See chapter 2 for instructions on flying a balloon with a burner (page 33).

Applying a fire retardant to the tissue paper will almost completely eliminate burn-ups on launching. If the wind catches the burner flame and pushes it onto the side of the envelope, all that will happen is the flame will scorch a hole through the tissue paper.

The easiest way to make a larger Khom Loi is simply to glue three sheets together instead of two in steps 1 to 5. This gives a Khom Loi that is about 6 feet (1.83 m) tall. The rest of the balloon is made in the same way.

You can also increase the lift in the balloon by making the diameter of the balloon bigger. Instead of gluing four panels together to make a 24-inch (60 cm) diameter envelope, you can glue five or even six panels together to make a 29-inch or 35-inch (74 cm or 89 cm) envelope. Because the diameter is so much larger, you will need to make a much larger pasted-together sheet for the circular top. Glue four sheets of tissue paper together as shown.

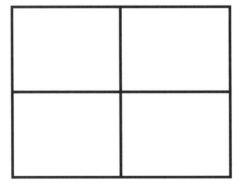

If you want to make the balloon fly for longer, you can wrap strips of aluminum foil around the string burner in between the string ties. This works by limiting the area of the waxed string that is exposed to burn. The wax in the shielded areas will melt and be fed into the flame by capillary action through the string fibers. You will have to experiment to see how much of the burner you can cover up before the lift is reduced too much.

If you want to fit a wire-free burner to the Khom Loi, you can use the design from chapter 6 (page 109).

8

The UFO Balloon

The UFO Balloon is a large, cylindrical balloon about 70 inches (178 cm) tall and about 25 inches (64 cm) in diameter. The top of the balloon is closed with a straight seam, like the bottom of a tube of toothpaste. This type of seam makes two points stick out like horns on either side of the balloon. The envelope is made from four flat rectangular panels, each made from three sheets of tissue paper glued together.

The bottom of the balloon is weighed down with a thick wire ring, bent around in a circle and simply held together with tape.

The envelope is very simple and quick to make and, as the large size and cylindrical shape means the envelope contains a lot of air, the UFO Balloon generates a lot of lift. The more lift the balloon can generate, the more fuel it can carry and the longer it can fly.

In the center of the ring is a special wax burner with 14 wicks and a wax reservoir that allows the balloon to fly for 20 minutes or more.

The Multiwick Burner

The cotton-ball burner commonly used on model balloons usually burns for around five minutes. If you make a cotton-ball burner larger it usually doesn't burn for a longer time, just with a larger flame.

Modern, full-sized, hot air balloons store pressurized gas in cylinders away from the burner and have valves to control the feed to the burners. Model balloons cannot use anything as heavy or complicated as that.

But you can use an idea taken from an old-fashioned oil lamp. The oil lamp stores the fuel in a separate tin and uses a simple wick to control the amount of oil that gets into the flame through capillary action. The thickness of the wick and length of the wick exposed to the flame determine how fast the fuel is burnt.

The multiwick burner works the same way. The burner has an upturned cup in the center that stops wax vapor from burning right off the surface, so that the wax is fed into the flame only by the wicks. Because the flame is only fed by the wicks, you can adjust the amount of lift and the flight time by changing the number and size of the wicks.

If you need to increase the lift, you can increase the number of wicks, choose a thicker string for the wicks, make the wicks a bit longer, or reduce the amount of wax in the burner (to reduce weight). If you want to increase the flight time, you need to reduce the number of wicks, make the wicks from a thinner string, cut the wicks a bit shorter, or fill the burner with more wax.

If you make the flame too small, or fill the burner with too much wax, then the balloon will not fly. A typical UFO Balloon should be able to lift about 2 ounces (60 g) of wax, and to get the air in the balloon hot enough, a typical multiwick burner uses up 1 ounce (30 g) of wax every 17 minutes.

History and Problems of Long-Duration Flight

Since the very first balloon flights, pilots have competed to see how far they can travel in a balloon. The first manned balloon flight was in a hot air balloon and covered about 5½ miles (8.8 km). The first flight in a hydrogen gas balloon took place only weeks later and covered 22 miles (35 km). Hot air balloons were much easier to control than the early gas balloons. To make a hot air balloon rise, you simply stoked up the fire to make it burn hotter. To make the balloon sink, you let the fire burn lower, or raked out the hot coals and allowed them to fall away.

Despite the fact that a hot air balloon was easier to control, it suffered from two major problems when it came to setting distance records. First, you have to be able to carry enough fuel to keep the balloon flying. The farther you want to go, the more fuel you need to carry. Second, early hot air balloons regularly set fire to themselves. Sparks and embers carried up into the envelope would settle on the fabric of the envelope and start small fires. In fact, Pilatre de Rozier, the pilot on the first manned balloon flight, had to bring the balloon down early; the envelope had almost divided in two as there were so many holes scorched through it. Without parachutes or any means of escape, this made early hot air balloons incredibly dangerous.

Early gas balloons were also dangerous. In addition to the hazard from a large volume of explosive gas in the envelope above the pilot's head, there were mechanical problems. Before reliable gas valves were designed, several balloons simply burst when they climbed too high. As a gas balloon flies higher into the atmosphere, the gas inside expands due to the reduced air pressure. The balloon pilot needs to release small amounts of gas to relieve the strain on the envelope. If the pilot does not do this or the gas valve jams, the envelope will rip apart.

Yet even if the valve is working, the pilot could release too much gas. The balloon would fall too fast, and the pilot would have to throw out sand ballast to slow the balloon down. If too much ballast is thrown out, then the balloon will start to rise again! Inexperienced balloon pilots could swing up and down releasing gas and ballast until either the envelope ripped or the balloon smashed into the ground.

De Rozier thought he had a solution. He combined the benefits of the gas balloon and the hot air balloon. He planned to cross the English Channel in a balloon that had two envelopes. On top there was a spherical gas balloon filled with hydrogen. The gas balloon was a bit smaller than normal, so that without any lift from the second envelope the balloon would descend slowly. The second envelope was a cylinder-shaped hot air balloon directly underneath the gas balloon. The idea was that the height of the balloon could be controlled by the hot air balloon in the usual way, but the amount of fuel needed would be greatly reduced, as most of the lift would be provided by the gas balloon.

Unfortunately, the design was a disaster. The attempt to cross the English Channel failed after only a few miles when the envelope caught fire. The hydrogen burst into flames and the whole balloon fell into the sea. De Rozier and all of the passengers died. After such a dramatic failure on its first flight, no one wanted to pursue de Rozier's ideas and no more Rozier-type balloons were made for nearly 200 years.

Gas valve designs improved, pilots became more experienced, and ballooning became safer. But one big problem still remained: you can't get a balloon to go where you want. It's blown by the wind.

When you want to travel really long distances, you run into a big problem with the wind. Most weather systems are circular—wind spirals into low pressure areas and spirals out of high pressure areas. Any balloon released into the wind will follow a complex path, changing direction as it passes from one weather system to the next. In theory a balloon could even travel around in a giant circle and arrive back where it started. This makes long-distance travel at low altitude pretty random.

The answer came with the discovery of the *jet streams*. Jet streams are very strong, high-altitude winds that blow from west to east all of the way around the world. For example, the northern polar jet stream flows across the top half of the United

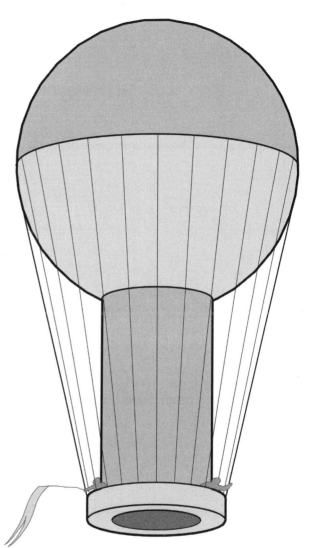

De Rozier's long-distance balloon

States at a height of between 23,000 and 39,000 feet (7.0 to 11.9 km). The actual position of the jet stream weaves and wanders about—it is farther north in the summer and shifts to the south in the winter.

Jet streams are caused by a combination of the heating effect of the sun and the rotation of the earth. The wind speeds are typically well above 100 mph (160 kph), and speeds of up to 247 mph (397 kph) have been measured. The jet streams are usually a couple of hundred miles wide but occupy a narrow band of altitude often less than 15,000 feet (4.6 km) from top to bottom.

But to travel in the jet stream you need a very special type of balloon. To keep the passengers alive, they need to be inside a pressurized cabin rather than an open basket. The balloon also needs to have precise control of altitude, even during the night.

Normally, gas balloons fly higher during the day as the sun warms the gas inside the envelope. When the sun sets, the gas cools and the balloon settles to a lower altitude. This would be a problem for a balloon riding in the jet stream. The balloon might drop too low and leave the bottom jet stream during the night and rise out of the top of the jet stream in the middle of the day.

To cope with the daily change in lift, long-distance balloon designers did two things. First, they improved the insulation of the balloon. They coated the envelope material with a layer of reflective aluminum. This reflected the heat of the sun during the day and meant that the gas warmed up more slowly. During the night the reflective layer also slowed down any heat loss from the gas, leading to much more even lift. They also made the balloons with a double skin, sometimes even blowing the air out from between the two skins during the day to keep the gas even cooler.

Second, they revived the Rozier balloon. Modern gas balloons use helium rather than hydrogen, and helium does not burn. Also, in a modern hot air balloon the hot air is generated using a propane burner. Propane burns very cleanly, producing just carbon dioxide and water vapor along with the hot air. This means that there are no embers or sparks to burn the fabric. Although the Rozier balloon still had to carry fuel for the burners, they needed much less than for a conventional hot air balloon. The hot air balloon part of the envelope gave pilots the control they needed to keep the balloon in the fast-moving air currents.

On March 1, 1999, Bertrand Piccard and Brian Jones took off from Château-d'Oex in Switzerland in a giant Rozier balloon called *Breitling Orbiter 3*. Almost 20 days later it landed in the Egyptian desert. They had travelled 25,361 miles (40,815 km) and completed the first nonstop trip around the world in a balloon.

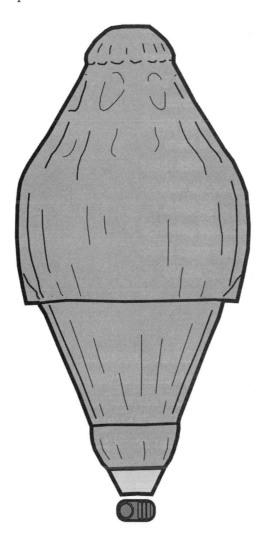

Breitling Orbiter 3

How to Make the UFO Balloon

Adult supervision required

Materials

12 sheets of tissue paper, 20 inches by
26 inches (50 cm by 66 cm) or larger

1 cup (240 mL) diluted white craft glue
(1 part PVA glue to 5 parts water)

5 feet (1.5 m) iron wire, 16 gauge
(1.6 mm diameter)

Thin clear tape, lightweight masking tape,
or similar

Aluminum foil

7 feet (2.1 m) thin iron garden wire

Rubbing alcohol (a little may be needed to
clean the wire)

Soft jute or cotton string

Tea light or nightlight

1 ounce (30 g) paraffin wax or beeswax

Tools

Narrow sponge or brush (to apply glue)

Ruler

Pen

Heavy books or food cans to keep the tissue
paper from moving

Scissors

Clean sponge and dry cloth

Pliers (with wire cutters)

8 small pieces of cardboard, ¾ inches by
2 inches (2 cm by 5 cm), to hold ring
in place

8 paper clips to hold ring in place

Strong plastic cup or glass with a 1½-inch
(38 mm) diameter base to use as former
for foil cup

Straight (dressmaker's) pin

Large jar, about 4 inches (10 cm) in diameter,
to melt wax

Heatproof gloves

Safety glasses

Before You Start

You will need a large, flat surface to build your balloon. You can use a table or the floor, but whatever you use you is going to get glue on it, so make sure the glue won't damage it. You can help to protect the table or floor by cutting trash bags into large plastic sheets to cover the work area.

If you do cover your table with plastic sheets, you can leave the balloon on the table to dry, as white craft glue will not stick to the plastic used to make trash bags. The balloon will dry more slowly if you leave it on the table rather than hang it up, but it is a lot easier.

As with any tissue paper balloon, it is a good idea to ***have the bottom 12 inches (30 cm) of the balloon coated with a fire retardant.*** You need to coat the tissue paper before you create the balloon—see chapter 11 (page 221) for instructions.

When you make a tissue paper balloon, most of your time is spent waiting for the glue to dry. If you have a blow-dryer, you can make a balloon much more quickly by using the blow-dryer to blow warm air at the glued seams. ***Don't use a fan heater or other room heater as they can set the tissue paper on fire.***

What to Do If Things Go Wrong

Holes in the tissue paper are easy to fix, and the UFO balloon will still fly well. You can find repair instructions in chapter 11.

In fact, check chapter 11 if you have accidentally glued parts of the panels that shouldn't be glued together, if you need a recipe for a different glue, if you cannot find the right materials, or if you have any other problems.

How to Make the Envelope

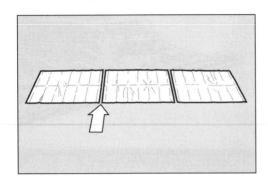

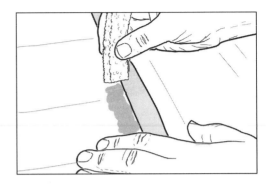

1. Put three of the tissue paper sheets on a large table or on the floor. Arrange them so they meet along their narrow edges. You are going to join the left-hand and middle sheets first.

2. Wet a narrow sponge (or brush) with diluted glue and squeeze it out so that it is nearly dry. Apply glue to the edge of the left-hand sheet of tissue paper as shown.

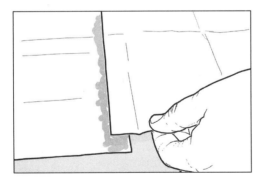

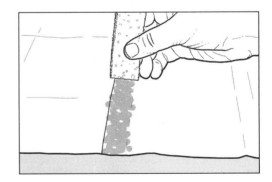

3. Lift the middle sheet of tissue paper across, line it up so it overlaps the glued edge by about ¾ inch (2 cm), and press down.

4. Apply more glue to the seam so that it soaks through both sheets. This will glue together any dry patches.

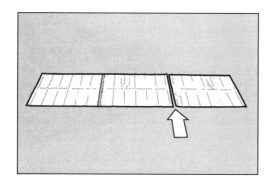

5. You will now join the middle and right-hand sheets.

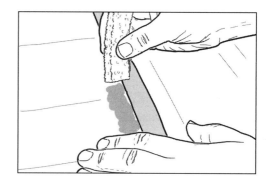

6. Apply glue to the edge of the center sheet as shown.

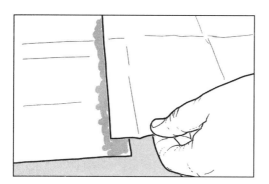

7. Lift the right-hand sheet of tissue paper across, line it up so it overlaps the glued edge by about ¾ inch (2 cm), and press down.

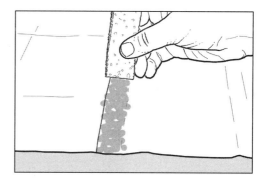

8. Apply more glue to the seam so that it soaks through both sheets. This will glue together any dry patches.

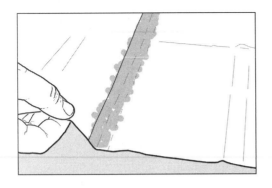

9. Gently life the left-hand sheet of tissue paper so that both seams peel away from the table or floor. Put the long tissue paper panel over the back of a chair or over the top of a door so that it can dry.

   Repeat steps 1 through 9 until you have four panels each made from three tissue paper sheets.

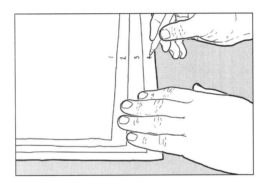

10. Number each panel in the order that you will assemble them. Remember to number alternating colors if you are making a two-colored UFO Balloon.

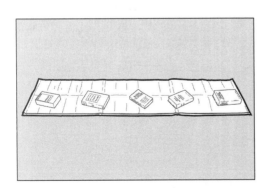

11. Lay panel 1 on the table or floor. Lay panel 2 on top and slide it away from you by ½ inch (13 mm) to expose a strip of panel 1 along the near side. Check that the exposed strip is even along its length and then put a few heavy books or food cans on top to keep the panels from moving.

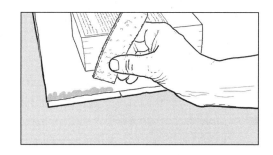

12. Make a series of cuts spaced 4 inches (10 cm) apart across the projecting strip of the lower panel. Make sure that you only cut across the projecting strip and not into the upper panel.

13. Wet a narrow sponge with diluted glue and squeeze it out so that it is nearly dry. Dab the sponge along the edge of the top panel to make a strip about ½ inch (13 mm) wide, wet with glue. If the sponge is too wet then excess glue will bleed sideways.

14. Take hold of the flap and fold it up onto the glued strip of the upper panel and pat it down.

15. Dab your sponge over the flap to stick down any dry patches. Continue with the rest of the flaps until you finish the seam. Peel the envelope off the table or floor and hang it over the back of a chair to dry. Wipe the glue from the work area with a clean sponge and dry with a cloth.

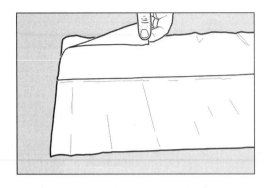

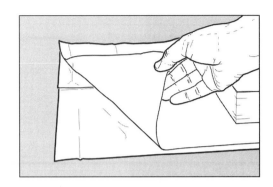

16. When the seam is dry, put the envelope back on the table or floor with panel 2 on the bottom. Make sure that numbered ends are on your right-hand side. Fold back the top panel (panel 1) so that the free edges line up with the seam at the back of the envelope. Make a neat crease down the middle. This puts panel 1 safely out of the way and leaves panel 2 exposed so it is easy to join to panel 3.

17. Lay panel 3 on top of the envelope and slide it away from you to expose a strip of panel 2 at the front that's ½ inch (13 mm) wide. Make sure that the strip is even along its length and put books or food cans on top to keep the panels in place.

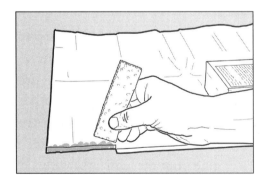

18. Make the seam just as you did in steps 12 to 15. Peel the assembly off the table or floor and hang over a chair to dry. Clean and dry the work area.

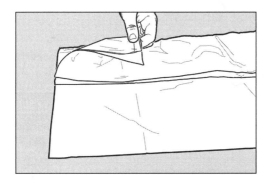 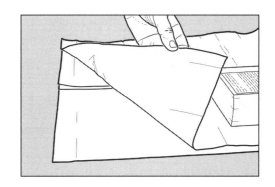

19. When the seam is dry, put the envelope back on the table or floor with
panel 3 on the bottom. Make sure that
numbered ends are on your right-
hand side. Fold back panels 1 and 2
so that the free edges line up with the
seams at the back of the envelope.
Make a neat crease down the middle.

20. Lay panel 4 on top of the envelope
and slide it away from you to expose
a strip of panel 3 at the front that's ½
inch (13 mm) wide. Make sure that
the strip is even along its length and
put books or food cans on top to keep
the panels in place.

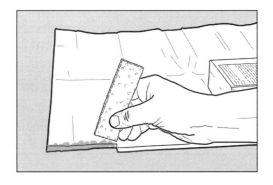

21. Make the seam just as you did in steps
12 to 15. Peel the envelope off the
table or floor and hang over a chair to
dry. Clean and dry the work area.

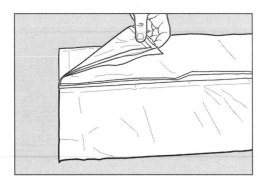

22. When the seam is dry, put the envelope back on the table or floor with panel 4 on the bottom. Make sure that numbered ends are on your right-hand side. Fold back panels 1, 2, and 3 so that the free edges line up with the seams at the back of the envelope. Make a neat crease down the middle.

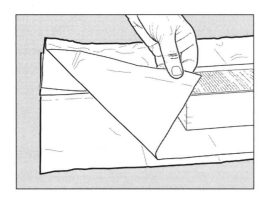

23. Take the edge of the top panel on the stack (panel 1) and fold it forward again over the bottom panel (panel 4). Line up the top panel to expose a strip of the bottom panel as you did before.

   This will be more difficult than before, as the back edge of the top panel is already joined to the envelope and will not slide easily. Use the heavy books to hold the top panel in place to expose an even strip of the lower panel, even if this means that the back edge of the top panel lifts and moves about. You may have to put a book close to the edge to hold it down so that you can glue it.

24. Form the seam as you did in steps 12 to 15. Peel the envelope off the table or floor, hang it up to dry, and clean the work area.

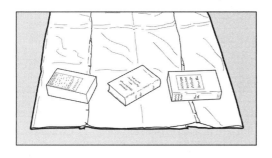

25. When the envelope is dry, flatten it out onto the table or floor so that there are no seams at the sides.

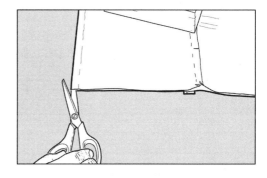

26. Cut slits 1 inch (25 mm) long at the sides of the envelope.

27. Fold back the top edge and glue the lower edge all the way along.

28. Fold the top edge back and press it down onto the lower edge.

29. Apply more glue to the seam so that it soaks through both sheets. This will glue together any dry patches. Make sure you glue together the sheets right up to the end of the slits at the side. Peel the envelope off the table or floor and hang it up to dry. Clean the glue from the work area.

How to Fit a Thick Wire Base Ring

30. When the envelope is dry, flatten it out onto the table or floor again so there are no seams at the sides and the remaining open end is toward you.

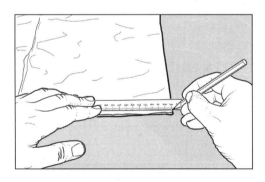

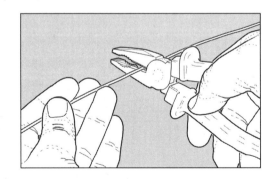

31. Measure across the open end of the envelope.

32. Cut a piece of thick wire twice as long as the distance measured in step 31.

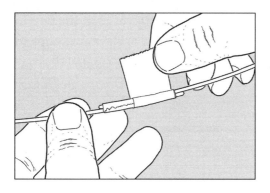

33. Clean the ends of the wire to remove any oil or grease that might prevent tape from sticking to it. If the wire is very oily, you may need to use a little rubbing alcohol. Bend the wire around in a circle. Overlap the ends by 2 inches (5 cm). Wrap two lengths of tape tightly around the overlapped ends. Lay the envelope on the table or floor and put the thick wire ring inside the opening at the base.

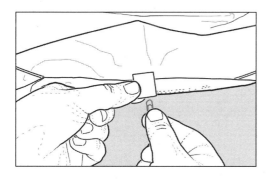

34. Fold ¾ inch (2 cm) of the lower edge of the opening over the thick wire ring, fold a small piece of cardboard over the tissue paper, and hold it in place with a paper clip.

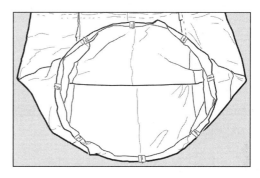

35. Repeat until there are eight paper clips evenly spaced around the thick wire base ring. Lay the envelope flat on the table or floor with the ring on top. Draw the lower edge toward you to ensure that none of the envelope is trapped underneath.

36. Tear the lower edge of the envelope between two of the paper clips to form a flap. Fold the flap down onto the table or floor and glue the tissue paper above the ring, as shown. Make sure that the glue doesn't stick the tissue paper to the cardboard fixing.

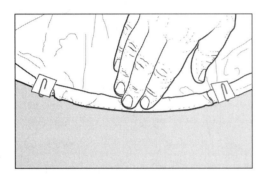

37. Fold the flap back up and pat onto the wet tissue paper.

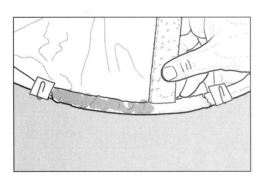

38. Rewet the flap to stick down any dry patches. Lift the envelope off the table or floor and clean the glue from the work area. Because the tissue paper gets very weak when it is wet, you should only glue alternate gaps between the fixings. You can glue the rest after the first gaps are dry.

    Hold the balloon up, turn it so that the next gap is toward you, and lay the balloon down onto the table or floor.

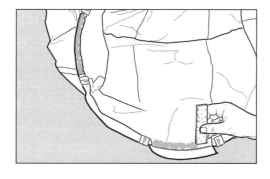

39. Tear down a flap and glue it as before. Lift the balloon up carefully and clean the glue from the work area.

    Repeat these steps until you have glued half of the gaps. Put the balloon to one side and prop the base ring up until the glued flaps are dry. Remove all of the cardboard fixings and paper clips.

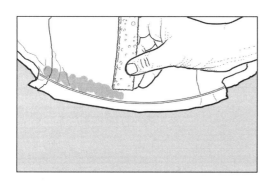

40. Glue the remaining flaps in the same way and put the completed balloon to one side to dry.

How to Make a Multiwick Burner

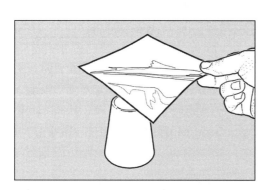

41. Cut a 6-inch (15 cm) square of aluminum foil. Put the center on the base of a small upturned glass or plastic cup and push the foil down the sides. The glass should have a base about 1½ inches (38 mm) in diameter.

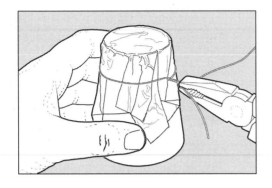

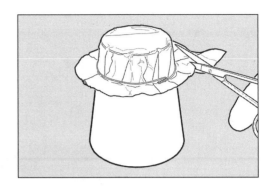

42. Wrap a length of thin wire around the foil about 1 inch (25 mm) from the base of the glass. Twist the ends of the wire together and bend the twist to lie alongside the ring.

43. Lift the bottom edge of the foil and spread it out into a horizontal skirt. Use a pair of scissors to trim the skirt so that it projects from the foil cup by only ½ inch (13 mm) all around.

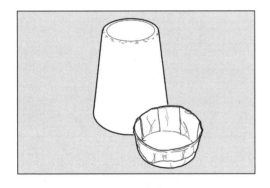

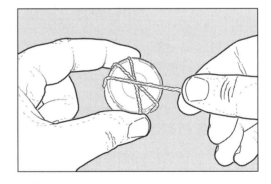

44. Fold the skirt up so the wire ring is trapped under the foil and smooth it onto the sides of the foil cup. Slip the foil cup off the glass and put it to one side.

45. Take a length of string and wrap it around a tea light seven times. Arrange the loops of string evenly around the tea light as shown.

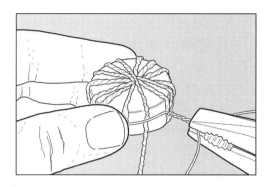

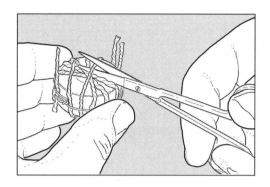

46. Hold the string tight against the tea light body and wrap a length of thin wire around the edge of the tea light. Twist the wire to trap all of the string loops into place. Cut off the excess wire and bend the twist to lie alongside the wire ring.

47. Use a pair of scissors to cut each loop as it passes across the middle of the bottom of the tea light. Adjust the cut ends of the string so that they all stand up.

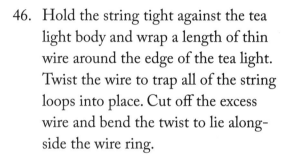

48. Prick the base of the tea light three or four times with a dressmaker's pin. Place the tea light into the foil cup that you made earlier. The original wick will be underneath the tea light and the cup of the tea light will be upside down. The strings bound to the sides of the tea light will form the new wicks.

Put some blocks of wax into a jam jar and **ask an adult** to help you melt it. You can find out how to melt wax safely in chapter 11 (page 219).

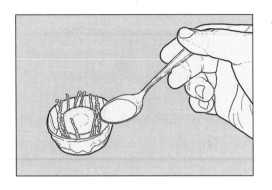

49. When the wax has melted in the jam jar, put on heatproof gloves and safety glasses and take the jar out of the oven. Spoon the wax into the foil cup, filling the gap around the tea light. Try to dribble wax over the string wicks so that they soak it up. Put the burner to one side so the wax can harden.

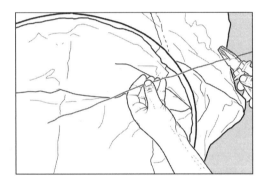

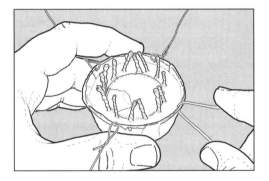

50. Take a length of thin wire and put one end at the center of the base ring. Cut the wire 4 inches (10 cm) beyond the side of the base ring. Repeat this so that you have four lengths of wire.

51. When the wax has hardened, take one of the wires and push the end through the foil just below the wire ring that makes the upper edge of the foil cup. Bend the wire back over the ring and twist the wire around itself. Repeat this so that there are four wires radiating out. Each wire is looped around the ring that forms the upper edge of the foil cup.

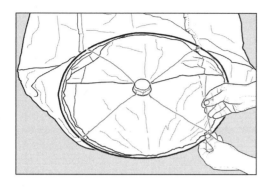

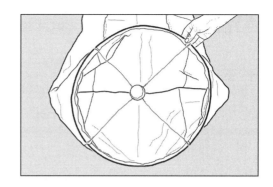

52. Put the burner upside down in the center of the base ring and arrange the wires evenly. Push the burner wires through the tissue paper next to the thick wire ring in the base of the envelope. Bend each burner wire so it loops over the base ring and twist the free end around the main part of the burner wire.

53. Cut off any excess from the burner wires to save weight.

What Next?

Check the envelope for any leaks by inflating it over an electric toaster or blow-dryer. Look for gaps in the seams or holes in the tissue paper and repair them (see instructions in chapter 11, page 211). *Take care that the hot air from the toaster does not melt the wax or it could spill from the foil cup and may set the toaster on fire.* Once you have fixed any leaks, the balloon is complete and ready to fly. See chapter 2 (page 33) for instructions on flying a balloon with a burner.

Applying a fire retardant to the tissue paper will almost completely eliminate burn-ups on launching. If the wind catches the burner flame and pushes it onto the side of the envelope, all that will happen is the flame will scorch a hole through the tissue paper.

Alternative Envelope Top

You can make a neater top to the UFO Balloon by cutting the panels to a point. Glue the tissue paper sheets together as described in steps 1 to 10 on pages 156–158.

1. After the panels have dried completely, lay all four of them in a stack on your table. Smooth the panels down and carefully line up their top and left-hand edges. Use four straight pins to hold the panels together at the corners.

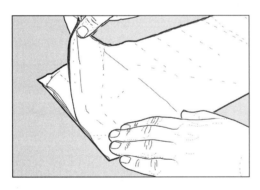

2. Fold the whole stack in half so that the long edges meet and the fold is toward you.

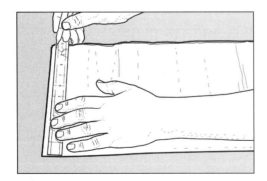

3. Measure the width of the left-hand end of the stack. If the panels don't quite line up, then measure to the narrowest panel.

4. Measure the same length along the far edge of the stack and make a mark. If the edges of the panels don't line up properly, then make the mark on the narrowest panel.

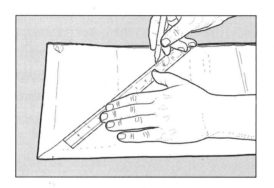

5. Draw a line connecting the left-hand corner of the fold to the mark you made in the previous step.

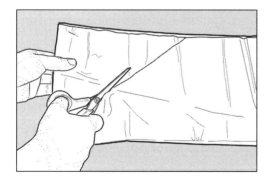

6. Cut along this line to remove a triangle of tissue paper. Open the panels, remove the pins, and continue with the envelope build from step 11. Skip steps 26 to 30, as the end of the envelope will already be closed by the pointed top. When you open up the envelope, the top will have a square shape like the Kongming Lantern.

Alternative Multiwick Burner

If you cannot find tea lights in your local store, you can make a great alternative multiwick burner out of cardboard and aluminum foil. You will need a mini stapler, foil, cardboard, scissors, string, and a straight pin.

Make the foil cup as described in steps 41 to 44 on pages 167–168. Cut a strip of cardboard ¾ inch (2 cm) wide from a cereal box.

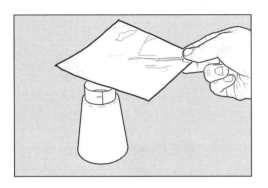

1. Cut and staple the cardboard into a ring ½ inch (13 mm) smaller in diameter than the base of the glass you used to make the foil cup. Place the ring on top of the glass and put a 5-inch (127 mm) square of aluminum foil on top.

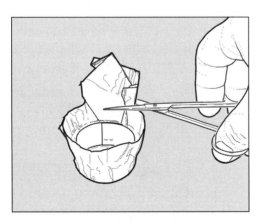

2. Push the foil down the sides of the glass and squeeze the foil onto the cardboard ring and glass to form another foil cup. Try to keep the ring circular. It doesn't matter that the foil won't lie close to the cardboard at this stage. Lift the foil cup and ring off the glass and turn it upside down. Trim the foil so a skirt of about ½ inch (13 mm) projects beyond the cardboard ring.

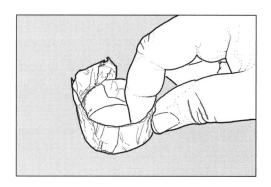

3. Fold the foil skirt inside the ring and squeeze the foil tight to the cardboard ring all around.

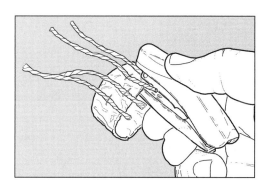

4. Cut 14 2-inch (5 cm) lengths of string and staple them to the side of the burner.

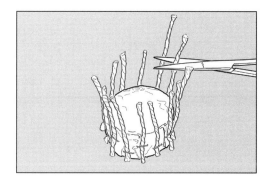

5. Trim one end of the string wicks so they are level with the open side of the burner, and trim the other end so they project above the closed end by about 1 inch (25 mm). Prick the closed end of the burner with a straight pin three or four times.

Filling the alternative multiwick burner with wax is easy. Grip the open edge of the burner carefully with a pair of pliers and dip the wicks into a jar full of molten wax to soak them. Set the burner aside to cool. Pour molten wax into the larger foil cup and lower the burner cup into place. Air should escape through the pricked holes and allow the burner cup to settle. Leave the burner assembly to cool and harden.

9

The Taped Solar Tetroon

The Taped Solar Tetroon is shaped like an upside-down triangular pyramid about 4 feet (1.2 m) tall, each edge being about 5 feet (1.5 m) long. The tetroon is made from four sheets of very thin black polyethylene cut from cheap plastic trash bags. The sheets are joined together using tape (clear tape is fine).

Because the envelope is made by just taping together plastic sheets cut from trash bags, the Solar Tetroon is very easy and quick to make. And of course, it just costs a few cents.

The Solar Tetroon has no burner. Instead, the air inside is heated by solar energy collected by the black plastic envelope. The tetroon has a small opening made by cutting off the corner of the envelope that points down, and there is a postcard attached to this opening. The postcard acts as a weight to keep the balloon upright (the warm air would escape if the envelope rolled over and the opening pointed upwards). But the postcard can also contain contact information.

Tetroons can travel for hundreds of miles, so you can't follow one after you launch it. I put an anonymous e-mail address (through Hotmail) on the postcard along with a few

words asking the person finding the balloon to contact me and let me know where he or she found it. That way I could figure out how far it traveled.

Of course, you can only launch solar-powered balloons when the sun is shining. It is no good if there are any clouds in the sky. If one passes in front of the sun, the Solar Tetroon will immediately start to lose height.

Tetroons

The name "tetroon" comes from a description of the shape—it is a tetrahedral balloon—a tetroon. Tetroons are used by scientists in many studies of the upper atmosphere because they are simple and very tough. It is easier to make a polyethylene or polyester tetroon that is tough enough to cope with high-altitude flight than to make a normal spherical balloon. The straight seams of a tetroon resist splitting much better than the curved seams of a spherical balloon.

These scientific tetroons are filled with a light gas, such as helium, and have a small package of instruments and transmitters suspended underneath. Because the electronic equipment needed to track a free-flying tetroon is now so cheap, amateurs have started to use tetroons to take high-altitude photographs of the Earth and are tracking their own tetroons as they travel around the world.

In the previous chapter (page 149) you saw that one of the problems you need to solve when making a long-distance hot air balloon is carrying enough fuel to keep the balloon up in the air. The UFO Balloon was large enough to carry a store of wax and control the burn using wicks, but the Solar Tetroon does not need to carry any fuel at all, since it uses the power of the sun to heat the air inside it. The Solar Tetroon does not need solar panels or complicated electronics like a solar-powered airplane; it simply absorbs sunlight because of the black color of the envelope. And because it is not limited by the amount of fuel that it can carry, the Solar Tetroon can easily travel very long distances.

Although the heating effect of the sun is very strong—about one kilowatt falls on the surface of the Solar Tetroon on a sunny day—most of the heat is lost straight to the atmosphere, so the air inside the tetroon does not get very hot. Luckily, because the Solar Tetroon needs no burner or base ring, it can be made very light. Lighter balloons need less lift before they will fly, and in a hot air balloon this means that the air does not need to get so hot. In the Solar Tetroon the air only needs to get about 20°C (36°F) warmer than the surroundings before it will fly. The air inside a black plastic bag sitting in the sun will easily get as hot as that, even if a lot of heat is lost to the atmosphere.

The envelope also needs to be as airtight as possible so that the hot air does not leak out. Tissue paper is not really suitable, as it always has small pinholes. This does not matter so much when you have a burner providing lots of really hot air, but a solar balloon cannot afford to lose any hot air at all. Black polyethylene used to make cheap trash bags is ideal, but you need to find the lightest ones that you can.

In fact, everything needs to be as light as possible. For example, you should use ordinary clear tape to join the plastic sheeting together and not duct tape, as duct tape is much heavier.

Because most people have never even heard of a solar-powered hot air balloon, I have included some answers to frequently asked questions—FAQs.

Solar Balloon FAQ

Is the sun strong enough to fly a solar balloon where I live?

The sun's strength varies depending on how far north or south of the equator you live. However, the amount of variation is less than you might think. According to NASA, on an average day in July the strength of the sunlight falling on the ground is 620 watts per square meter in Seattle and 630 watts per square meter in Miami. Because you need less than 500 watts per square meter to fly a Solar Tetroon, you can fly one anywhere in the mainland United States.

Can I fly a Solar Tetroon in the winter?

Yes you can. Although it gets cold in the winter, the sun will still warm the air inside the envelope. A hot air balloon works because the air is warmer than the surrounding air, so when the surrounding air is cold, the air in the balloon doesn't have to get very hot before the balloon will fly.

You might think that the sun is weaker in the winter, and so the Solar Tetroon will not work as well, even though the air doesn't have to get as warm. In fact, if the sky is completely clear, the strength of the sun is very nearly the same in winter and summer. The average sun strength falling on the surface of a Solar Tetroon launched at midday in Central Park, New York, would be:

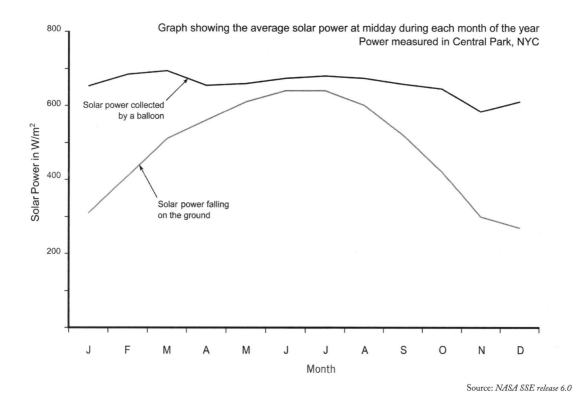

Graph showing the average solar power at midday during each month of the year
Power measured in Central Park, NYC

Source: *NASA SSE release 6.0*

This shows that the power from the sun is pretty constant in strength throughout the year. The reason that it is colder in the winter is not because the sunlight is weaker, but because the days are shorter and the Earth is tilted farther away from the sun, making the sunlight spread out over a larger area of ground.

Will the Solar Tetroon fly better in the summer?

Although you can fly the Solar Tetroon in the winter, it will fly farther in the summer. This is simply because the days are longer in the summer. A Solar Tetroon will fly only as long as there is daylight. As soon as the sun starts to set, the balloon will start to fall. But in the summer this means that if you launch early in the morning, you can have a flight of 10 hours or more, and the balloon can cover hundreds of miles.

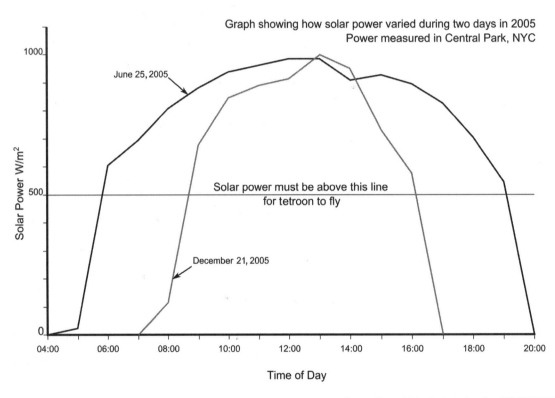

Graph showing how solar power varied during two days in 2005
Power measured in Central Park, NYC

June 25, 2005

Solar power must be above this line
for tetroon to fly

December 21, 2005

Source: *National Solar Radiation Database (USAF#725033)*

If a particular design of Solar Tetroon needs 500 watts per square meter to fly, you can see that if you launch a Solar Tetroon from New York's Central Park in June, the sun is strong enough for the balloon to fly between 5:30 AM and about 7:00 PM. In December the sun is only strong enough for the tetroon to fly between about 8:30 AM and 4:00 PM. That means in June you could have a flight of up to 13½ hours, compared with a flight of 7½ hours in December. Of course, 7½ hours is still a very long flight!

What time of day is best for launching?

Early morning is usually best. If the sky is clear, then the sun should be strong enough to heat the Solar Tetroon as soon as it has completely risen above the horizon. It is often a bit less windy just after dawn as well. And of course, you want to launch as early as you can to get the longest flight time.

Does weather affect the Solar Tetroon?

The Solar Tetroon will not work if there are even thin clouds covering the sun. This means that you shouldn't launch if there are any clouds in the sky. When the tetroon is flying low, any thin cloud passing in front of the sun will make the tetroon start to fall. Once the tetroon has been flying for a while, it will climb above the clouds and will continue to fly however many clouds start to form below it.

Rain will weigh down the envelope and drive it to the ground, and the rain clouds will also block the light.

Because the Solar Tetroon is so light, it is carried along at the same speed as the wind, and so the tetroon can cope with quite high winds. Because the tetroon is traveling at the same speed as the wind, the envelope will not be cooled down at all by air movements. However, high winds can make it very difficult to launch the Solar Tetroon, and you will need a large, open area to allow the tetroon to climb to a safe height as it is carried down-wind. Gusty wind can cause problems for the tetroon: the return tag at the bottom of the balloon needs to be heavy enough to keep the tetroon stable, and the opening at the bottom of the envelope needs to be small so that hot air is not lost when the tetroon is blown about.

How do I know if the sky is clear enough?

In many places it can be hard to know if the haze in the sky is thick enough to block the power of the sun and stop the Solar Tetroon from flying. Because the actual solar power depends on the weather, tables or charts can't tell you what time or which day to launch. The easiest way to find out if the Solar Tetroon will fly is to use a simple solar power meter. You can make one for yourself in about 10 minutes. All you need is an extra black plastic trash bag, two thermometers, some string, tape, cardboard, and a clear plastic bag. There are instructions in chapter 2 (page 24).

Where will it go?

Like any balloon, the Solar Tetroon will be carried in the exact direction that the wind is blowing. The difference is that the tetroon can fly for so long that it can pass through several weather areas. You can get a general idea of where the tetroon will go if you look at the weather map on the evening before you launch. If you live on the coast, you don't want to launch when the wind will be blowing out to sea—no one will pick up your return tag and contact you.

How to Make the Taped Solar Tetroon

Adult supervision required

Materials

4 lightweight black plastic trash bags
    (the thinnest you can find—see chapter
    11, page 215)
Thin clear tape, lightweight masking tape,
    or similar, ¾ or 1 inch (19 mm or
    25 mm) wide
Postcard
Small plastic sandwich bag

Tools

Scissors
Pen

Before You Start

The Solar Tetroon is very easy to build; the only difficulty is finding somewhere to build it! The tetroon is too big to build on most tables, so I build mine on the floor. To make the tape connections in these really large sheets, you will need to hold down the sheets with small pieces of tape. This can damage some types of wooden floors, so ask first.

You're going to have to walk on the envelope while you build it, so take off your shoes. Because thin polyethylene will often stick to bare feet, you should wear socks. Sweep any dirt or grit off the floor or it may damage the thin polyethylene.

If you can't find lightweight trash bags or if you have any other problems, check chapter 11 (page 215) for advice. In particular, if you make small holes in the plastic sheet or there are small gaps in the seams, see chapter 11 (page 213) to find out how to fix them.

If you get the tape in the wrong place, do not try to unpeel it, as you will just tear the plastic sheet. Complete the seam as best you can and put another length of tape over the gap.

How to Make the Envelope

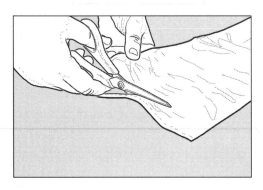

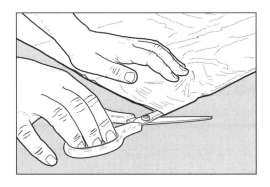

1. Carefully cut off the closed end of a black plastic trash bag. Cut as close to the weld as you can. (The weld is the melted line running straight across the bottom of the bag.)

2. Cut a slit up the side of each trash bag to make a large rectangular sheet. Use the folds in the bag as a guide to keep the cut straight.

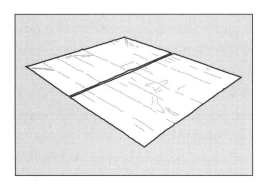

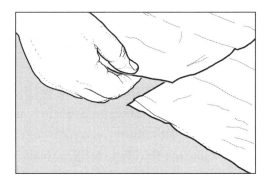

3. Place two sheets side by side on the floor so that the long edges touch.

4. Overlap the edges by ¾ inch (2 cm).

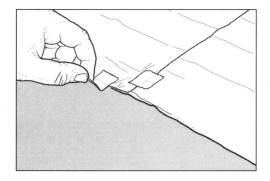

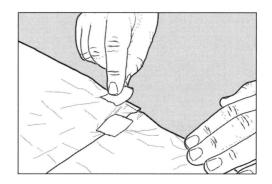

5. Put a small piece of tape across the seam at one end and attach the sheets to the floor with a second piece of tape.

6. Pull the other side of the seam to straighten the edges and hold them in place with a short piece of tape. Secure the sheets to the floor with another piece of tape.

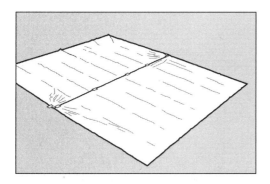

7. Check that the overlap is the same in the middle of the sheet and put three or four more pieces of tape on the seam to keep everything straight.

8. Attach the end of a roll of tape to the floor just beyond one end of the seam. Unroll about 12 inches (30 cm) of tape and line it up over the seam. Keep the tape straight but don't pull so hard that the tape stretches. Lower the tape over the seam and carefully smooth it down.

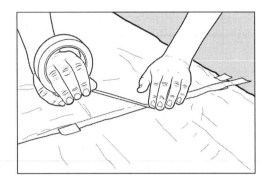

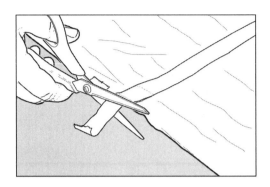

9. Keep the stuck-down length of tape in place with one hand and unroll another 12 inches (30 cm) of tape with the other. Line this up over the next section of the seam and lower the tape onto the seam. Smooth it down. Continue until the entire seam is taped.

10. Lift the tape off the floor and trim it close to the edge of the sheet with a pair of scissors. Fold any remaining stub of tape under the sheet.

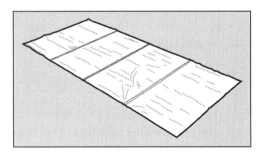

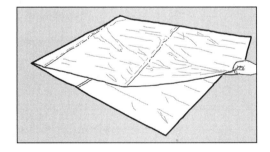

11. Add the third and fourth sheets by repeating steps 4 to 10. You should now have a long sheet of black plastic made from four trash bags, all joined together by their long edges.

12. Turn the sheet over so that the taped seams are on the underside.

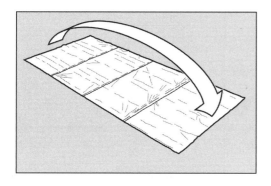

13. Lift the left-hand edge up and across to fold the sheet in half as shown.

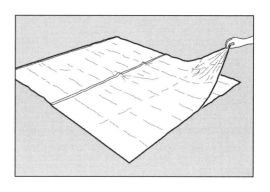

14. Line up the edges carefully.

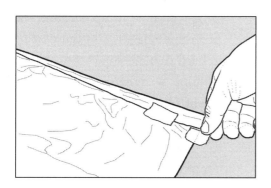

15. Fold over ¾ inch (2 cm) of both edges at the back right of the sheet as shown. Hold the fold in place near one end with a small piece of tape, and secure the sheet to the floor using a second piece of tape.

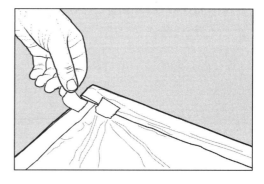

16. Straighten the folded seam by gently pulling at the other end and use a piece of tape to hold the fold down. Tape the end of the seam to the floor using another small piece of tape.

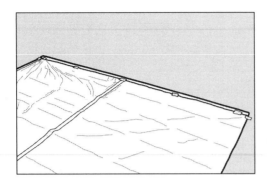

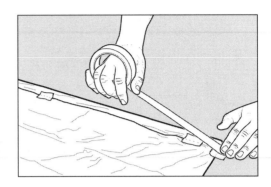

17. Check that the fold is the same in the middle of the sheet and put three or four more pieces of tape on the seam to keep everything straight.

18. Attach the end of a roll of tape to the floor just beyond one end of the seam. Unroll about 12 inches (30 cm) of tape and line it up over the seam. Keep the tape straight but don't pull so hard that the tape stretches. Lower the tape over the seam and carefully smooth it down.

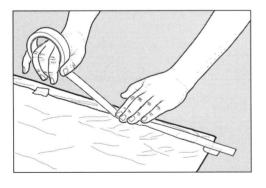

19. Keep the stuck-down length of tape in place with one hand and unroll another 12 inches (30 cm) of tape with the other. Line this up over the next section of the seam and lower the tape onto the seam. Smooth it down. Continue until the entire seam is taped.

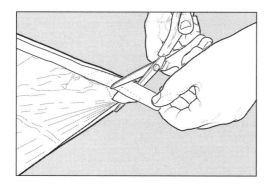

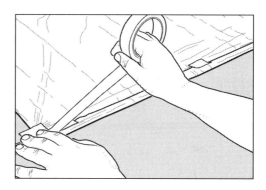

20. Lift the tape off the floor and trim it close to the edge of the sheet with a pair of scissors. Fold any remaining stub of tape under the envelope.

21. Fold up the edges at the front right of the envelope as shown, and make a taped seam in the same way as you did in steps 15 to 20.

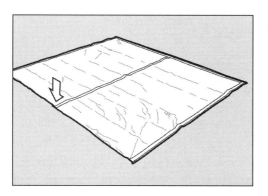

22. The only remaining open edge should now be the front left as shown. You need to reposition the envelope so that the final folded seam is made at right angles to the seam on the opposite side. This will give the balloon a triangular pyramid shape rather than a fat pillow shape.

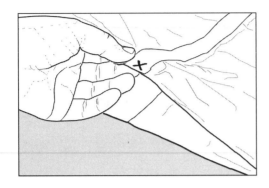

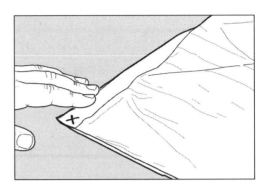

23. Lift the envelope by the two seams in the center of the open edge.

24. Pull these two seams apart and put the envelope back on the floor with these two seams now at opposite ends of the open edge.

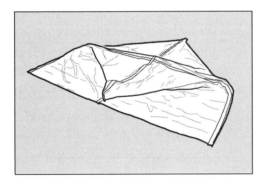

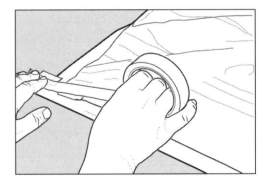

25. This will put the open edge at right angles to the back right edge of the envelope as shown.

26. Fold up the open edge and make a taped seam in the same way as you did in steps 15 to 20.

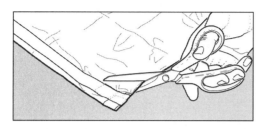

27. Flatten out the completed envelope and pull one corner toward you. Cut the corner off using a pair of scissors. You should aim to make the opening about 3 to 4 inches (75 to 100 mm) in diameter.

You should now inflate the envelope with a blow-dryer and check the seams to make sure that there are no gaps. Repair any gaps or holes with small pieces of tape.

How to Make a Return Tag

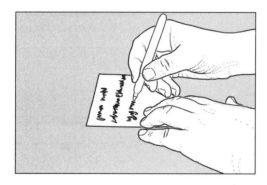

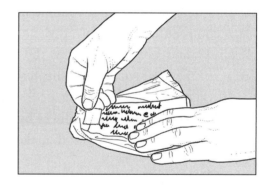

28. Write your contact details on the postcard.

29. Turn a small clear plastic sandwich bag inside out and tape the postcard to the side of the bag near the sealed end.

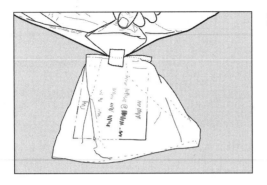

30. Turn the bag right side out again and tape the sealed end of the sandwich bag to the opening at the bottom of the Solar Tetroon. With the opening of the sandwich bag pointing down, any condensation or rain drops will run off and the postcard will not get wet.

What Next?

Inflate the envelope indoors with a blow-dryer so you can check the seams for any gaps that might leak warm air. If you find any gaps or holes in the envelope, you can find instructions on repairing polyethylene envelopes in chapter 11 (page 213). Once you have checked it and repaired any holes, the tetroon is ready for flying. You will find instructions on launching solar balloons in chapter 2 (page 39).

If you can find trash bags made from very thin polyethylene but they are smaller than 29 inches wide by 35 inches tall (74 by 89 cm), you can still use them but you will have to tape more of them together to make a tetroon. Tape them into one of the patterns on page 195 or 196.

If you can find big lightweight trash bags but you just want to make a Solar Tetroon with more lift (that will fly later on into the sunset), you can make either a Welded Solar Tetroon (page 197) or a larger Taped Solar Tetroon.

The Solar Tetroon in this chapter is formed by joining four polyethylene sheets together in a row:

This is because the sheets you get from most trash bags are about twice as wide as they are tall. When you lift the left-hand edge over to fold, the row in half the envelope ends up almost square, making a regular tetrahedron. The tetroon doesn't have to be a regular tetrahedron with each edge exactly the same. You can tape six sheets together in a row:

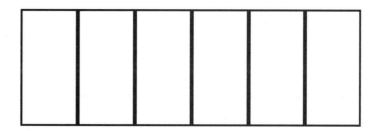

When you fold the left-hand edge over, you get a tetroon that looks "stretched" but has a lot more lift than the regular four-sheet tetroon. You can tape together nine sheets like this:

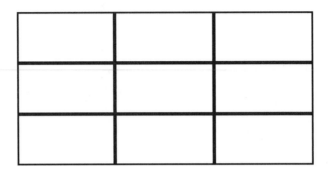

And when you fold the left-hand edge over, you get a very large regular tetroon. The edges are 50 percent longer than those of the four-sheet tetroon, and this tetroon has a lot of lift. Finally, you can tape 16 sheets together in this pattern:

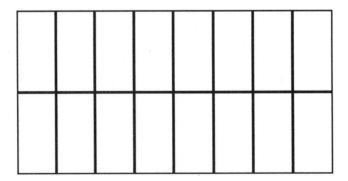

When you fold over the left-hand edge and tape up the sheets, you get a regular Solar Tetroon that in theory could lift a payload of almost 2½ pounds (almost 1.13 kg).

10

The Welded Solar Tetroon

The Welded Solar Tetroon is shaped like an upside down triangular pyramid about 4 feet (1.2 m) tall, with each edge about 59 inches (150 cm) long. The tetroon is made from four sheets of very thin black polyethylene cut from cheap plastic trash bags. The sheets are welded together using a regular soldering iron.

The Welded Solar Tetroon is very simple, but welding the sheets takes a little practice. Welding holds the polyethylene sheets together with an airtight seam without the need for tape. The Taped Solar Tetroon weighs about 3 ounces (85 g), and ½ ounce (14 g) of this is the tape. Because the Welded Solar Tetroon is the same size and shape but ½ ounce lighter, under the same conditions it has more lift and will fly for a longer period. (And of course a welded envelope costs even less than a taped one—around 18 cents each.)

The tetroon has no burner, as the air inside is heated by solar energy collected by the black plastic envelope. The tetroon has a small opening made by cutting off the corner of the envelope that points down, and there is a postcard attached to this opening. The postcard acts as a weight to keep the balloon upright. (The warm air would escape if the

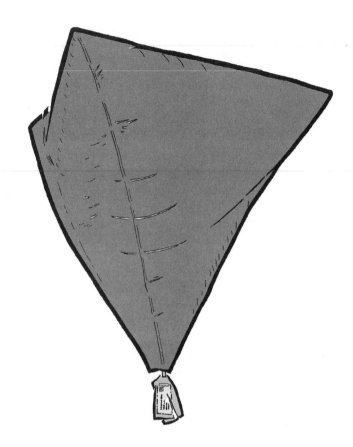

envelope rolled over and the opening pointed upward.) The postcard can also contain contact information.

Tetroons can travel for hundreds of miles, so you can't follow one after you launch it. I put an e-mail address on a postcard card along with a few words asking the person finding the balloon to contact me and let me know where he or she found it. That way you can figure out how far it traveled.

Of course, you can only launch solar-powered balloons when the sun is shining. It is no good if there are any clouds in the sky. If one passes across the sun, the Solar Tetroon will immediately start to lose height.

History of Solar Balloons

In 1965, Howard Bauerson filed a patent describing a hot air balloon made from light-weight polyethylene. The clever part of his patent was that this hot air balloon did not need a burner to keep it in the air. The polyethylene contained a black dye (just like cheap trash bags), and the black polyethylene would absorb enough of the sun's rays to warm the air inside. The air would only be warmed by about 15°C (27°F) compared to the surrounding air; a normal hot air balloon heats the air by 70°C (126°F) or more. But because the envelope was made with such a low-weight polyethylene sheet, the 15°C temperature rise would be enough to get the balloon to fly.

Bauerson's patent described small balloons, intended as toys or as distress markers, and it is clear from the patent that he only intended to make balloons less than 6 feet (1.8 m) in diameter.

On May 16, 1973, Tracey Barnes made the first manned solar-powered balloon flight. Barnes was a professional balloon designer and had already produced novel designs of conventionally powered hot air balloons. Barnes's solar balloon was a giant black monster, several times larger than a normal "sport" balloon. It was made with conventional hot air balloon technology: it was stitched together from black rip-stop nylon. It had to be big to get enough lift to carry a passenger, as the temperature rise was very low.

Although the materials and manufacture were conventional, the shape was definitely not. Rather than the usual teardrop shape, this balloon was an upside-down tetrahedron, which is a pyramid with a triangular rather than a square base—just like the balloon in this chapter. Barnes's basket was attached to one point of the tetrahedron.

Barnes probably chose a tetrahedron as the surface area is larger than for a teardrop balloon of the same volume. Normally a large surface area is bad, as it makes for a balloon that loses heat quickly, but Barnes wanted the maximum surface area available to collect sunlight. Although Barnes flew the balloon as a pure solar balloon at first, he quickly decided that it would be a lot safer to fit a burner. If you have a burner, you won't crash when the sun goes behind a cloud.

One problem with a simple black solar balloon is that only half of the collected solar energy is used to heat the air inside. The inside of the balloon skin heats up the air inside, but the heat from the outside of the balloon skin is lost to the atmosphere.

A number of inventors have produced designs to fix this problem, and all of them work in a similar way. To make sure all of the energy is collected, they have a clear outer envelope and some sort of black collector suspended inside.

In 1981, Julian Nott flew one of these improved solar balloons across the English Channel. He flew from Dover to Calais, and the whole flight took only two hours. The balloon was designed by Dominic Michaelis, and it had a clear plastic outer envelope with a smaller black balloon inside, which acted as the collector. Because of the lower heat rise, it was still a good deal larger than a normal hot air balloon, but due to the improved efficiency it was smaller than Barnes's earlier balloon. Nott had fitted a propane burner for emergency use, but once the balloon was filled and had lifted off the ground, the balloon collected solar energy so well that he didn't have to use the burner at all.

Most solar balloons use polyethylene rather than rip-stop nylon and are much smaller than Barnes's balloon. They carry payloads in grams rather than hundreds of kilograms, and owe a lot more to the designs of Bauerson than to those of Barnes or Michaelis. However, in one respect they often resemble Barnes's balloon: many homemade balloon builders make tetrahedral balloons. This is probably because tetroons, as they are known, are so easy to make. If you start with rectangular sheets of polyethylene then you don't even have to cut them to shape; you can just tape them together.

You can buy model solar balloons from a number of science toy websites. They are usually tubular balloons 3 meters (10 feet) long, just under 1 meter (3 feet) in diameter, gathered in and clipped at the ends.

The instructions to launch the balloon are very simple. You gather one end together and clip it shut with a cable tie. Then you hold the other end open and walk forward to fill it with air. When it is full you close the end, twist, and clip it shut. Then you lay the balloon on the ground in the full sun. Eventually the air inside will warm up enough so the whole thing rises into the air.

How to Make the Welded Solar Tetroon

Adult supervision required

Materials

4 lightweight black plastic trash bags
(the thinnest you can find—see chapter
11, page 215)
Thin clear tape, lightweight masking tape,
or similar, ¾ or 1 inch (19 mm or
25 mm) wide
Postcard
Small clear plastic sandwich bag

Tools

Scissors
Long plank of wood to provide a smooth welding
surface (and protect the floor from heat)
Heavy books or food cans to keep the plastic
sheet in place
Metal ruler
30-watt soldering iron with a pointed or screw-
driver tip
Soldering iron stand
Small damp sponge to clean melted plastic
off the tip and barrel of the soldering iron
Pen

Before You Start

You should not use a soldering iron without careful adult supervision. If you haven't used one before, ask someone to show you how to handle it safely. And if you're still uncomfortable with it, have an adult helper perform the welding steps.

If you can't find lightweight trash bags or if you have any other problems, check chapter 11 (page 215) for advice. In particular, if you make small holes in the plastic sheet or there are small gaps in the seams, see chapter 11 (page 213) to find out how to fix them.

If you get the tape in the wrong place, do not try to unpeel it, as you will just tear the plastic sheet. Complete the seam as best you can and put another length of tape over the gap.

How to Make the Envelope

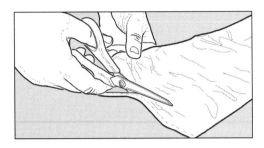

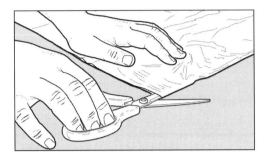

1. Carefully cut off the closed end of a black plastic trash bag. Cut as close to the weld as you can. (The weld is the melted line running straight across the bottom of the bag.)

2. Cut a slit up the side of each trash bag to make a large rectangular sheet. Use the folds in the trash bag as a guide to keep the cut straight.

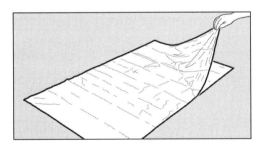

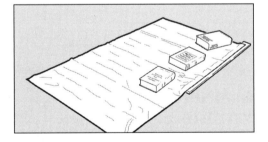

3. Place two sheets on the floor with one on top of the other.

4. On the right-hand side, line up the long edges of the sheets and put the wooden plank underneath so that the edges run down the middle of the plank. Put four or five heavy books or food cans on top to keep the sheets from moving around.

5. Lay the metal ruler on top of the wooden plank so that ¼ inch (6 mm) of the plastic sheet projects from underneath the metal ruler. Put the soldering iron in its stand and switch it on. When it is hot, place the tip against the metal ruler just beyond the plastic sheet.

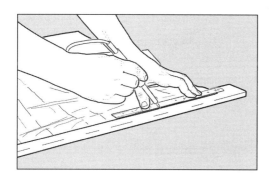

6. Hold down the metal ruler with one hand and slowly draw the pointed tip along the edge of the ruler. The soldering iron can only weld about 1 inch (25 mm) of sheet per second, so go slowly. If you are using a screwdriver-tipped soldering iron, hold the iron at an angle to use just one of the corners of the tip. As you drag the tip through the plastic sheet, the heat will cut through it, leaving a thin ribbon of waste on one side and welding the two sheets together on the other side. Lift the soldering iron before you reach the end of the ruler.

Don't worry if the ribbon of waste melts onto the barrel of the soldering iron. Use a damp sponge to quickly wipe it away by holding the sponge at one end and using the other end to wipe the soldering iron. This keeps your fingers well away from the hot parts of the iron. Keep the sponge damp and never hold the sponge still against the soldering iron—keep it moving.

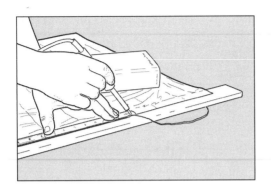

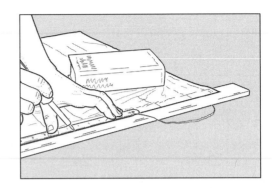

7. Reposition the metal ruler so that one end lines up with the weld and the other lies ¼ inch (6 mm) away from the unwelded edge of the sheet. Place the tip of the soldering iron against the steel ruler.

8. Draw the iron along the metal ruler again to weld another section. Continue until the whole edge is welded. Unless your plank is very long, you will have to reposition it at least once.

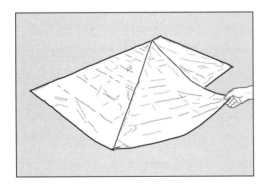

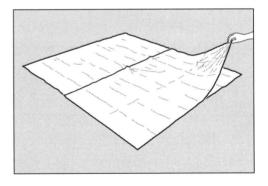

9. Open up the pair of plastic sheets.

10. Lay a third sheet on top and line up the front right edges carefully. Put the wooden plank under the front right edges.

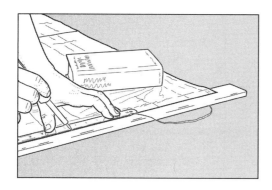

11. Weld the edges of the sheets as you did in steps 5 to 8. Repeat until you have four sheets welded together.

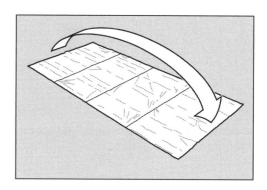

12. Take the left-hand edge of the row and lift it over the rest of the sheets to line up with the right-hand edge of the row, folding the whole envelope in half.

13. Line up the back right edges of the envelope. Put heavy books or food cans on top of the plastic sheet to keep it from moving and put the wooden plank under the free edges.

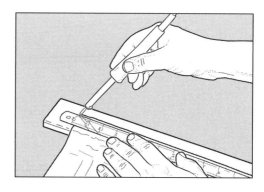

14. Weld the edges together as you did in steps 5 to 8.

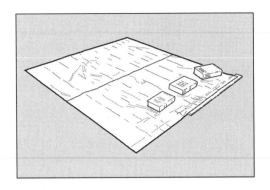

15. Place the plank under the front right edges of the envelope.

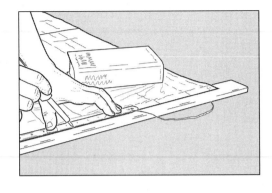

16. Weld the front right edges together as you did in steps 5 to 8.

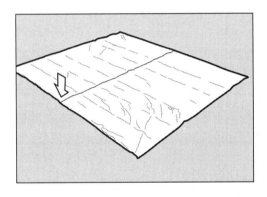

17. The only remaining open edge should be the one at the front left, as shown. This needs to be repositioned so that the last weld forms the envelope into a tetrahedron rather than a fat pillow shape.

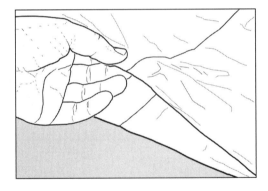

18. Hold the envelope where the welds meet the middle of the open edges.

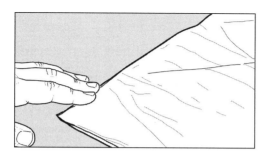

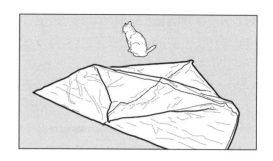

19. Lift the envelope and pull these middle welds apart. Put the envelope back down with these middle welds now at either end of the open edge.

20. The envelope should now look something like this.

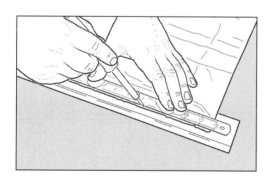

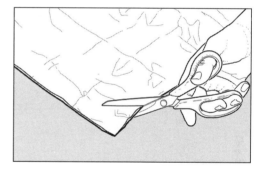

21. Put the plank under the open edges and weld them together as you did in steps 5 to 8.

22. Flatten out the completed envelope and pull one corner toward you. Cut the corner off with scissors. You should aim to make the opening about 3 to 4 inches (75 to 100 mm) in diameter. Inflate the envelope with a blow-dryer and check the seams to make sure that there are no gaps. Repair any gaps or holes with small pieces of tape.

How to Make a Return Tag

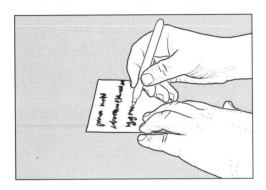

23. Write your address on a postcard, put a stamp on it, and add your email address if you have one. The person finding your balloon is more likely to contact you if you make it easy for him or her. If you don't want to use your private email address, you can sign up for a free Hotmail account and use that instead.

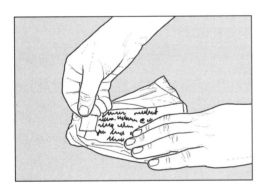

24. Turn a small sandwich bag inside out and tape the postcard to the side of the bag near the sealed end.

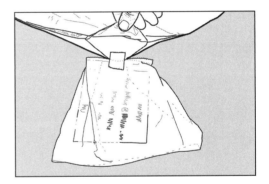

25. Turn the bag right side out again and tape the sealed end of the sandwich bag to the opening at the bottom of the Welded Solar Tetroon.

What Next?

Inflate the envelope indoors with a blow-dryer so you can check the seams for any gaps that might leak warm air. If you find any gaps or holes in the envelope, you can find instructions on repairing polyethylene envelopes in chapter 11 (page 213). Once you have checked it and repaired any holes, the tetroon is ready for flying. You will find instructions on launching solar balloons in chapter 2 (page 39).

If you want to make a tetroon with more lift, see the "What Next?" section at the end of chapter 9 (page 194).

Because solar balloons fly for hours and don't carry a burner, you can launch them tethered to the end of a long line, a bit like a kite. Unlike a kite, you can only fly a tethered solar balloon on a still day without any wind. Wind will carry a free balloon along with it, but a tethered balloon is stationary and the wind chills the air inside. The wind can even push the balloon back to the ground.

The line used to tether a Welded Solar Tetroon needs to be as light as possible. Fishing line (monofilament nylon) is a good choice as it is light, strong, and waterproof. For the tetroon in this chapter, you don't need a very strong line—a 10-pound (4.5 kg) breaking strain should be fine. If you make larger tetroons or other large solar balloons, you may need to buy a heavier line.

Nylon fishing line is so slippery and springy it is difficult to knot. To make a loop at the end of the tether line, you need to tie a figure of eight loop. Make the loop at least 3 or 4 inches (75 or 100 mm) so that it is easy to tie and easy to attach to the envelope with tape.

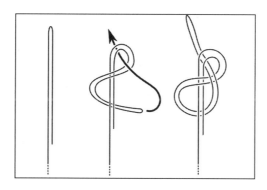

Once you have formed a loop, attach the tether line to the opening of the tetroon. Cut an 8-inch (20 cm) piece of tape and pass 1 inch (25 mm) through the loop. Fold the end of the tape back on itself so that it sticks and traps the loop. Stick the rest of the tape to the polyethylene so the loop in the tether line lies level with the opening in the envelope.

Giant Solar Sausage

If you can find thin and really big trash bags, you can make a tubular balloon like the ones you can buy on science toy websites. It is one of the simplest solar balloons around. All you do is cut the ends off 10 trash bags and tape them into a long tube by following the instructions in steps 10 to 24 of chapter 4 (pages 59–62).

Because the balloon will be so big, *you should only fly it on a tether*, and it will only work on a clear, bright day with no wind.

To fill the balloon, hold the edges of the open end apart and walk forward. The tube should fill with air. When the tube is full, close the open end and gather the edge together. Wrap a cable tie or a piece of tape around the gathered edge, seal it, and attach the tether line with another piece of tape.

Lay the balloon in full sun. After a few minutes the balloon will stir and eventually start to rise.

11

Troubleshooting and Other Information

This chapter contains extra hints and tips to help if you run into trouble while making the balloons in this book. In addition to advice on what to do if things go wrong, you will also find recipes for glue, suggestions for different base ring materials, and more.

Repairing Holes and Tears in Tissue Paper Balloons

Holes and tears in a tissue paper envelope can let out a lot of hot air and reduce a balloon's lift. This means it is very important to patch even small holes.

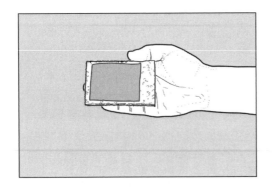

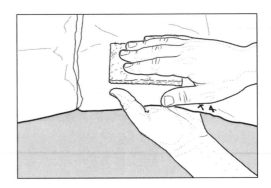

1. Cut a patch of tissue paper at least 1 inch (25 mm) larger than the hole or tear. Soak a large sponge in diluted white craft glue (PVA glue) and squeeze it so the sponge is just damp. Lay the tissue paper patch onto the sponge and gently press it down so the paper is soaked with glue.

2. Put your hand inside the envelope and support the tissue paper behind the hole with your palm. Press the sponge over the hole so the tissue paper patch transfers onto the envelope, and peel the sponge off the envelope, so that the patch stays in place.

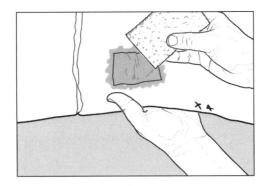

3. Use the corner of the sponge to gently push down any parts of the patch that did not stick to the envelope on the first try. Put the balloon to one side to dry.

Repairing Holes and Gaps in Polyethylene Balloons

Small holes in both taped and welded polyethylene balloons can be sealed using tape. Line up the edges as closely as possible before you press the tape into place. *If you stick the tape down in the wrong place, leave it there.* Do not try to remove it; you will make a much bigger hole in the polyethylene!

To patch a large hole, cut a rectangle of polyethylene and tape it over the hole. Make sure that the pieces of tape cross over each other at the corners so that the patch doesn't leak.

Small gaps in a welded seam can be repaired with tape, but longer gaps are best repaired by re-welding the whole seam.

Lay the envelope on the floor with the seam you need to repair lying flat and at the side of the envelope. Pull the seam straight, place a wooden board under the seam, and weld a new seam ¼ inch (6 mm) inside the old one.

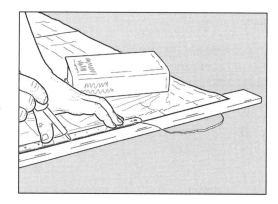

Mixing Glue

The easiest way to mix white craft glue (PVA glue) and water is to pour the glue into a clean jam or jelly jar up to a level of about ½ inch (13 mm) from the bottom. Top up to a level of 3 inches (75 mm) with water from the bottom. Put the lid on and shake the contents together.

Unscrew the lid. Cut two 6-inch (15 cm) squares from a polyethylene bag and place them over the neck of the jar. Screw the lid back on, trapping the plastic in between the top of the jar and the lid. The polyethylene squares will prevent the lid of the jar from getting stuck by the glue.

Rice Glue

If you cannot buy PVA glue where you live, or you would just prefer to make your own glue, you can make a very good glue from rice flour.

Materials
1½ cups (360 mL) cold water
Small saucepan
3 tablespoons (40 mL) rice flour
3 tablespoons (40 mL) sugar
3 tablespoons (40 mL) salt

Pour the cold water into a small saucepan. Stir the water while you sprinkle or sieve the ingredients into the saucepan. Heat the water until it boils, stirring constantly. Keep stirring while it boils for another 30 seconds to thicken. Allow the mixture to cool, then transfer it to a clean jam or jelly jar. Cut two 6-inch (15 cm) squares from a polyethylene bag and place them over the neck of the jar. Screw the lid on, trapping the plastic in between the top of the jar and the lid. The polyethylene squares will prevent the lid of the jar from getting stuck by the glue.

Wheat Glue

You can also make a very good glue from wheat flour.

Materials

2 cups (470 mL) cold water
Small saucepan
Heaping tablespoon flour
1 teaspoon (5 mL) sugar
½ teaspoon (2.5 mL) ground cloves or cinnamon

Pour the cold water into a small saucepan. Stir the water while you sprinkle or sieve the ingredients into the saucepan. Heat the water until it boils, stirring constantly. Keep stirring while it boils for another 30 seconds to thicken. Allow the mixture to cool, then transfer it to a clean jam or jelly jar. Cut two 6-inch (15 cm) squares from a polyethylene bag and place them over the neck of the jar. Screw the lid on, trapping the plastic in between the top of the jar and the lid. The polyethylene squares will prevent the lid of the jar from getting stuck by the glue.

Finding the Right Plastic Sheet

Polyethylene sheeting for hot air balloons needs to be as light as possible. The lightest sheets usually come from cutting up the *cheapest* polyethylene bags, because they are made from the thinnest plastic. Unless you have special measuring tools, like a micrometer, you won't be able to measure the thickness of the polyethylene bags at your local supermarket. To be sure, you will just have to buy a roll of bags and weigh them to see if they are light enough. Once you have handled one of the very thin plastic bags, it is much easier to tell which bags are likely to be thin enough. They feel limp and look blotchy when you hold them up to the light.

Unfortunately, you cannot tell by how much light passes through—manufacturers put more black dye into the thin bags to make them look thicker.

Sheet materials like paper and plastic sheet are often graded by the weight of a standard sheet size rather than by thickness. In the metric system, paper and plastic sheets are graded by the number of grams that a square meter of sheet would weigh.

For a solar balloon you need to use polyethylene sheet that weighs less than 12 or 13 grams per square meter. To figure out what grade of polyethylene sheet you have, weigh a trash bag on accurate weighing scales and divide this weight by the total area of sheet for the bag. To make the weighing more accurate, you can weigh 10 bags at a time and then divide the weight by 10 to get the weight of one bag.

Example Sheet Calculation

My supermarket sells trash bags that are 0.85 m tall and 0.75 m across the flattened opening. Ten bags weigh 144 g, so one bag weighs 14.4 g. When you slit open a trash bag and unfold it, the sheet is twice the size of the bag, so the area of sheet you get from one bag is $2 \times 0.85 \times 0.75 = 1.28$ m². One bag weighs 14.4 g and has an area of 1.28 m², so the grade of sheets is $14.4 \div 1.28 = $ *11.3 grams per m²*.

Finding the Right Tissue Paper

To make a model hot air balloon, you need to use very lightweight paper. Lighter paper makes a lighter balloon, which means more lift. But the paper cannot be made so thin that the hot air will leak through it. The very lightest papers often have many small holes all over, and these allow a lot of air to leak through.

Tissue paper is available pretty much anywhere—wherever gift wrapping paper is sold—and this is ideal for making model hot air balloons. It is light in weight but doesn't have too many holes. Tissue paper is sold in cut sheets measuring 20 inches by 30 inches, 20 inches by 26 inches, and 18 inches by 28 inches. If you have a choice, get the largest size, as a bigger balloon always has more lift.

Paper is usually graded by weight rather than thickness, and the grade is usually figured out by listing how much a standard size of sheet would weigh. The metric system is commonly used, where the paper is graded by the number of grams that a one square meter sheet would weigh. Tissue papers range from 14 grams per square meter to just under 18 grams per square meter. Cheaper brands of tissue paper are usually around 14 grams per square meter, and these are the ones to buy, as the balloon will be lighter and fly better.

Most manufacturers will print the weight of the paper somewhere on the packaging, but if they don't, it is easy to figure it out. You need to weigh a sheet of paper and then divide this weight by the area of the sheet. To make the weighing more accurate, you can weigh 10 sheets at a time and divide the weight by 10 to get the weight of one sheet.

Example Sheet Calculation

Ten sheets of my tissue paper weigh 46.3 g, so each sheet weighs 4.63 g. Each sheet is 0.5 m by 0.66 m (20 inches by 26 inches). The area of one sheet is $0.5 \times 0.66 = 0.33$ m^2. The paper grade is therefore $4.63 \div 0.33 =$ *14 grams per m^2*.

Finding the Right Base Ring Cane

Rattan—calamus, or simply "cane"—is an ideal material for making Khom Loi base rings and can also be used for any of the larger balloons. It is biodegradable and should not harm livestock if they eat it (after your balloon lands). Rattan is cheap and used commercially to make many woven products like baskets, boxes, and even chairs and tables.

Rattan comes from a vine grown in tropical countries and is very flexible when fresh, so it is easily bent around into a ring just using your hands. You can buy rattan from companies that supply basket-making materials or furniture repair materials. The vine is cut into several different parts that are all used for different parts of the basket and furniture-making process. What you want is called "center cane," which is the round pith from the middle of the vine. Buy center cane about ¼ inch (6 mm) in diameter. If you can only get dried cane, you will need to soak it in water for about 20 minutes just before you want to use it so it is flexible.

Split bamboo also makes excellent base rings. If you are lucky, you may be able to buy split bamboo as loose lengths; otherwise, you will have to split your own using a special tool shaped like a star that is hammered into the end of a bamboo rod. If you cannot find a splitting tool, you may be able to find discarded products like roller blinds and screens that are made from lengths of split bamboo. Use strips of bamboo no wider than ¼ inch (6 mm) or the base ring may be too heavy. Join the ring together by overlapping the bamboo strips and binding at two places using thin wire or fishing line in the same way as the rattan cane base ring in the Khom Loi project. You can even use tape.

One balloon builder I know recommends making a hoop by taping together split bamboo food skewers. If you can buy cheap packs of skewers, this might be worth trying. Depending on how thick they are, you may need to split them again down their length with a sharp knife. Overlap the ends and tape tightly to join.

Willow and rushes could also be used as material for base rings. Like cane, you may have to soak dried willow rods before they will be flexible enough to bend around into a base ring. If you want to gather your own willow, do this in the fall when the tree has stopped growing. Strip the bark off the rods and leave them to dry in a well-ventilated area. Cut off the thin tip and the highly curved butt end and overlap the rods when binding them together.

Finding the Right Wax

The easiest way to get paraffin wax for solid fuel burners is to buy cheap candles and melt them down; nightlights and tea lights are now so cheap that melting them down is almost as cheap as buying big blocks of wax from candle-making suppliers. As well as being very cheap, paraffin wax is easy to melt down and soaks into string fibers easily.

Beeswax burns with a brighter and slightly hotter flame than paraffin wax and produces a bit less soot. However, beeswax is much more expensive than paraffin wax. You can sometimes buy big blocks of beeswax from companies that supply furniture polishes and other wood finishing products. The beeswax is sold for craftsmen to make their own wax polishes.

Melting Wax

You should NEVER melt wax without adult supervision.

The easiest and safest way to melt wax is to use a microwave oven. The microwaves can't heat the wax itself, so you will have to use a water bath. Put 1 inch (25 mm) of water into a soup bowl and put about 2 ounces (60 g) of wax into an empty jam jar and place it in the bowl. A 900-watt microwave should be able to melt the wax in five or six minutes. *Use heatproof gloves to hold the jam jar—it will be very hot—and wear safety glasses to protect your eyes in case the wax splatters.* Swirl the jam jar every minute to mix the wax and check the level of water. If the water gets very low, add boiling water from a kettle.

Don't put the water in the jam jar along with the wax. The mixture will explode and coat the inside of your microwave with sticky globs of melted wax that are hard to scrape off. (Don't ask me how I know.)

If you don't have a microwave, you can ask an adult to melt the wax in a small pan on the stove. Put 1 inch (25 mm) of water in the bottom of the pan and rest the jam jar in the center. It is very important that the water is not too deep and that the water only simmers gently or the jam jar might tip over. If the molten wax spills into the water, the wax can be thrown out by the bubbling water. If the wax does spill into the water, turn off the power and clean up after the pan has cooled down. *Use heatproof gloves and wear safety glasses when handling the jar of hot wax.*

Never melt wax in a standard electric convection oven. Even if you set the temperature to 100°C (212°F), the heating element will get much hotter than this. Wax vapor only needs to get to around 200°C (392°F) before it ignites. Wax that is producing wispy smoke is very close to catching fire.

I have melted wax in a fan-assisted electric oven without setting fire to my house (so far). The fan should keep the heating element cooler, but you must keep a careful watch on the wax and *turn the oven off as soon as you see any smoke*.

Don't ever try to melt wax in a gas oven.

If at any time the wax starts to burn, you should turn off the power and put a lid on top of the pan or container. After a short while the wax will stop burning when all of the air is used up inside the container. *Do not pour water onto burning molten wax*—cover it with a fire blanket. Let everything cool down before you clean up.

Finding the Right Wire

In many burners, the support wires sit within the burner flame itself. To stop the wire from burning through, the support wires should be made from iron or steel. Copper electrical wires are unreliable and often burn through.

You can buy soft iron wires from hardware and gardening stores. Gardeners use iron wire to tie up plants and to bind bamboo sticks into frames. Because it is used outside, iron wire is often zinc coated (galvanized) or plastic coated to stop it from rusting. Buy the zinc-coated wire if you can, as the plastic coating will burn.

You cannot use music wire or piano wire as it is too hard and snaps when you bend it.

Wire is often sold in sizes from various wire gauge systems. The wire is given a number rather listing the actual diameter. In the United States, the National Wire Gauge is used for ferrous wire (iron and steel), and the American Wire Gauge is used for nonferrous wire (everything else). In the UK, the Standard Wire Gauge system is used for both:

Standard Wire Gauge

SWG	mm	inch
26	0.45	0.018
24	0.56	0.022
22	0.70	0.028

SWG	mm	inch
20	0.90	0.035
18	1.20	0.048
16	1.60	0.064

For the purposed of making balloons, the National Wire Gauge and Standard Wire Gauge are pretty much the same size (the diameters are only very slightly different). AWG wires are nonferrous, and most will have too low a melting point to use as reliable burner wires (the sizes are also quite similar to SWG for this range).

The ideal iron wire for burner wires is 22- or 24-gauge (0.7 mm or 0.56 mm diameter)—strong enough but not too heavy. The ideal iron wire for the thin wire base ring used on the Kongming Lantern is 22-gauge (0.7 mm diameter). It is also a good size for binding the Khom Loi rattan base ring when making the overlap seams.

For the thick wire base ring you could use any type of metal wire that you can find. Thick, galvanized steel wire can be bought from farming supply shops, as steel wire is used for repairs to many types of fencing. A good size for the UFO Balloon is 16-gauge (1.6 mm diameter) steel wire.

Fire Retardant

If you search online, it is easy to find companies that will sell you aerosols and spray packs of fire retardant. If you get the right type, it can work well on tissue paper. Fire retardants don't prevent the burner flame from scorching holes through the paper, but they do stop the paper from catching fire. Unfortunately, the packs can be quite expensive.

The good news is that it is easy to make your own. I have listed two different fire retardants below. Because the Alum Fire Retardant is a bit cheaper, that's the one I use. You can buy the ingredients at a pharmacy:

Alum Fire Retardant

3 ounces (85 g) alum
½ pint (240 mL) hot water

Borax Fire Retardant

3½ ounces (99 g) borax
1½ ounces (42 g) boric acid
1 pint (470 mL) hot water

To make up the solution, just dissolve the ingredients in the hot water, allow to cool, and store in a labeled jar or bottle. If the solution gets cold, some crystals may form in the bottom of the jar. Gently heat the solution again and the crystals will re-dissolve.

You only need to apply the solution to the lower 12 inches (30 cm) of the tissue paper sheets to protect from the burner flame. Before you start, mark one end of the sheet with an X to show which end has been treated.

1. Use a sponge to spread the fire retardant solution onto one half of the tissue paper sheet. (Note the marked X.)

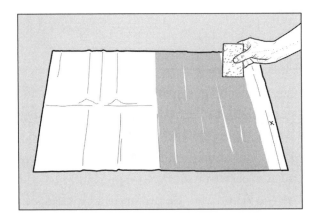

2. Hold the dry corners on the untreated half and peel the tissue paper off the table. Use a clothespin to hang the sheet on a washing line or similar, so that the wet half can hang down to dry.

Repeat for as many sheets as you need. For example, the Kongming Lantern would need four treated sheets; the panels should be glued together so that the treated parts are at the bottom, next to the burner flame.

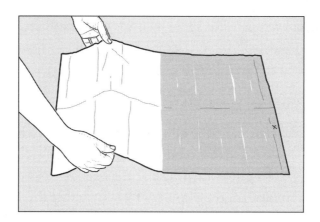

Fixing the Fire Balloon That Won't Fly

The balloon designs in this book have been tested to make sure that they fly well, but sometimes things can go wrong and a balloon refuses to take off. Usually this is quite easy to fix.

Is it too heavy?

When you are choosing the materials to make your balloon, always try to get the lightest ones you can. The thickness of the paper makes a big difference to the overall weight, as does the thickness of the wire. If you have poured too much kerosene onto the cotton-ball burner, don't worry—you'll just have to wait for a couple of minutes after you light the burner for the extra kerosene to burn off.

Always use diluted glue for the envelope, as straight white craft glue is much heavier.

Are there any holes?

Holes in a balloon will let the hot air leak out. Just a few holes can cut enough lift to stop the balloon from flying. Use an electric toaster or blow-dryer to inflate the balloon and carefully check over each panel to spot any holes or tears. Check along each seam to make sure that they are glued all the way across. If you find any holes, then patch them as described in the section at the start of this chapter.

Is the burner flame too small?

If the string used to make your multiwick burner is too thin, then the burner may not produce enough heat. The size of flame produced by the multiwick burner depends on the number, thickness, and length of the wicks. If the balloon does not generate enough lift, then you may need to increase the number of wicks so that the burner generates more heat.

Similarly, if you make a cotton-ball burner out of a ball that is too small, then the burner flame will be too small to heat the air inside the balloon and the balloon will not lift off the ground.

Is there any wind?

In addition to causing problems with the burner flame blowing against the sides of the balloon, wind can chill the air inside the balloon and greatly reduce lift. Even a small amount of wind will cool the balloon enough to slow down the initial climb rate. Try to shield the balloon from as much wind as possible. If you are in a large open area and the wind is very light, you could try walking downwind, holding the balloon up by the base ring until it starts to lift more strongly.

Fixing the Solar Balloon That Won't Fly

The solar balloon designs in this book have been tested to make sure that they fly well, but sometimes things can go wrong and a balloon refuses to take off. Usually this is quite easy to fix.

Is it too small?

The Solar Tetroon needs to be big to work. For a Taped Solar Tetroon, the trash bags need to be at least 34 inches (86 cm) deep by 29 inches (74 cm) wide. This makes a plastic sheet about 34 inches (86 cm) by 58 inches (1.47 m). If you can only find smaller trash bags, you may be able to make a working tetroon but you will need to make it out of more than four trash bags. See the "What Next?" section in chapter 10 (page 209).

Is it too heavy?

The Solar Tetroons are very sensitive to extra weight. The air inside the balloon heats up to only about 30°C (54°F) above the surrounding air, so there is not a lot of extra lift available. The Solar Tetroons won't work at all if you make them from regular, thick trash bags; you need to find much thinner ones—see the "Finding the Right Plastic Sheet" section in this chapter (page 215).

The tape used to join the Taped Solar Tetroon needs to be very light as well. Cheap (thin) ¾- or 1-inch masking tape works well, as does ¾- or 1-inch standard clear tape. Duct tape and thick or reinforced tapes are much too heavy.

The return card and sandwich bag together should weigh about ¹/₁₀ ounce (3 g). The card should be thin—3-inch-by-5-inch (75 mm by 127 mm) index cards are ideal.

Are there any holes?

Because there is so little lift in a solar balloon, it is important to check over the envelope to make sure that there are no holes to let the hot air out. Inflate the tetroon indoors using a blow-dryer and carefully check all of the seams to see if there are any gaps. Check the rest of the surface for small tears and cuts. Repair any holes (see the section at the start of this chapter).

Are there any clouds?

Even quite thin, wispy clouds can cut the heating power of the sun. If there are patchy clouds, this can be a problem for the first part of the flight. Until the balloon climbs above them, clouds passing in front of the sun will immediately make the solar balloon descend. Keep a check on the heating power of the sun with the solar power meter described in chapter 2 (page 24).

Is the opening too big?

If the opening in the corner of the envelope is too big, then gusts of wind can pump warm air out of the envelope by collapsing the sides. The tetroon will fall until the sun can warm the air inside again.

An opening of 4 inches (10 cm) is ideal. Any smaller and it is difficult to fit a blow-dryer into the opening. Any larger and you may lose warm air in gusty wind.

If you cut the opening too large, you can tape up part of it as shown below. Check that the balloon is stable by inflating it with a blow-dryer. If you have removed a lot of sheet from the corner, you may have to make the return tag a little bit heavier.

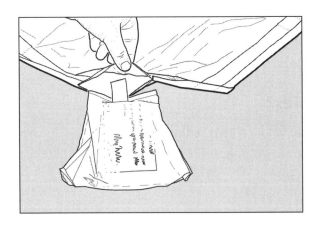

Is there any wind?

Even a small amount of wind will cool the balloon enough to cut the lift completely. Try to shield the tetroon from as much wind as possible. If you are in a large open area and the wind is very light, you could try walking downwind holding the tetroon. Keep the opening closed with one hand until the tetroon starts to lift.

If you believe the sun is strong enough but the breeze is chilling the balloon, you can jump-start the Solar Tetroon. See chapter 2 (page 39) for details.